ORTHO'S

Patio Plans

WITHDRAWN

Writers: Sharon Ross, Barbara Sabella
Illustrators: John Teisberg, Shawn Wallace, and Tony Davis

Meredith® Books
Des Moines, Iowa

Ortho® Books
An imprint of Meredith® Books

Ortho's Patio Plans
Solaris Book Development Team
Publisher: Robert B. Loperena
Editorial Director: Christine Jordan
Managing Editor: Sally W. Smith
Acquisitions Editors: Robert J. Beckstrom,
    Michael D. Smith
Publisher's Assistant: Joni Christiansen
Graphics Coordinator: Sally J. French
Editorial Coordinator: Cass Dempsey

Meredith Book Development Team
Project Editor: Benjamin W. Allen
Art Director: Tom Wegner
Copy Chief: Catherine Hamrick
Copy and Production Editor: Terri Fredrickson
Contributing Copy Editor: Carl A. Hill III
Technical Proofreader: Raymond L. Kast
Contributing Proofreader: Colleen Johnson
Electronic Production Coordinator: Paula Forest
Editorial and Design Assistants: Judy Bailey, Kaye Chabot,
    Treesa Landry, Karen Schirm, Kathleen Stevens
Production Director: Douglas M. Johnston
Production Manager: Pam Kvitne
Assistant Prepress Manager: Marjorie J. Schenkelberg

Additional Editorial Contributions
Editor: Jeff Day
Writer: Barbara Sabella

**Additional Editorial Contributions from
    Art Rep Services**
Director: Chip Nadeau
Designer: Laura Rades
Illustrators: John Teisberg, Shawn Wallace

Meredith® Books
Editor in Chief: James D. Blume
Design Director: Matt Strelecki
Managing Editor: Gregory H. Kayko

Director, Sales & Marketing, Retail: Michael A. Peterson
Director, Sales & Marketing, Special Markets:
    Rita McMullen
Director, Sales & Marketing, Home & Garden Center
    Channel: Ray Wolf
Director, Operations: George A. Susral

Vice President, General Manager: Jamie L. Martin

Meredith Publishing Group
President, Publishing Group: Christopher M. Little
Vice President, Consumer Marketing & Development:
    Hal Oringer

Meredith Corporation
Chairman and Chief Executive Officer: William T. Kerr

Chairman of the Executive Committee: E.T. Meredith III

Photographers
Laurie Black, 6, 10
John Holtorf, cover, 1
Susan M. Lammers, 9B
Michael Landis, 3B, 3T, 5, 9T, 34
Michael McKinley, 8
J. Parker, 15
Kenneth Rice, 11
Jeff Williams, 7

All of us at Ortho® Books are dedicated to providing you
with the information and ideas you need to enhance your
home and garden. We welcome your comments and
suggestions about this book. Write to us at:
Meredith Corporation
Ortho Books
1716 Locust St.
Des Moines, IA 50309–3023

Note to the Readers: Due to differing conditions, tools,
and individual skills, Meredith Corporation assumes no
responsibility for any damages, injuries suffered, or losses
incurred as a result of following the information published
in this book. Before beginning any project, review the
instructions carefully, and if any doubts or questions remain,
consult local experts or authorities. Because codes and
regulations vary greatly, you always should check with
authorities to ensure that your project complies with all
applicable local codes and regulations. Always read and
observe all of the safety precautions provided by
manufacturers of any tools, equipment, or supplies,
and follow all accepted safety procedures.

PLANNING A PATIO 4

BUILDING A PATIO 16

PATIO PLANS 34

4

PLANNING A PATIO

At its simplest level, a patio is nothing more than an outdoor pavement near a house. But a patio becomes less simple as you prepare to build it. Numerous questions arise. Where should it be located? How big should it be? What activities will it be used for? What special features do you want to include? How will it tie in with the overall property? What will it look like? Will it contain other structures? What should it be made of? And, finally, how do you build it?

This book helps answer those questions. The first part explores the design criteria for a successful patio. The second part describes basic patio construction techniques for the do-it-yourselfer who is ready to try some simple masonry.

The third part offers 14 patio plans designed for a wide variety of situations. Although all plans are for 18-foot by 30-foot patios or an equivalent area (540 square feet), the plans can be enlarged or reduced as needed, and the structures that go with them can be modified or moved from one design to another.

When designing a patio, keep in mind that it can be much more than a rectangular slab of concrete. Here, the patio functions as an outdoor seating area and an entry point to the inviting yard beyond. The site, materials, and design are all deliberate choices to enhance this patio's visual interest. It has both sunny and shady areas, uses irregularly shaped slate, and includes flower beds.

DESIGN GUIDELINES FOR A SUCCESSFUL PATIO

Curves used in this patio's design give it a natural look. Furniture also adds to a patio's look. Here, a round table and pots reinforce the curves of the patio's design.

A successful patio is an attractive place to enjoy the outdoors. It provides convenient, comfortable seating. It has a nonslip surface that doesn't get too hot for bare feet and doesn't reflect harsh, glaring light when the sun is overhead. It can provide shade, when needed, or maximum exposure to the sun, if desired. And, it is built of materials that stand up well to the elements.

Beyond those basic features, a patio is essentially an outdoor room that expands the living space of a home beyond its walls. As such, it should have many of the same attributes as an indoor room: privacy and enclosure, adequate size, easy access, physical comfort, and visual harmony.

PRIVACY AND ENCLOSURE

Most people don't want to feel as though they're on public display, when they're relaxing at home. The patio should be effectively screened from the street and from the neighbors.

You can provide privacy by placing your patio where existing features screen it. Possible sites include the least exposed side of the house, a corner where the main house meets a wing, behind a retaining wall or hedge, or in a grove of trees away from the house. Open patios that are a distance from neighbors may be private enough without

screening, as are hillside patios set above any neighbors. If the site doesn't have existing or natural screening, you can provide it by adding a fence, a retaining wall, or landscaping to your plan.

To provide a sense of enclosure, you might choose to define the borders of your patio with benches, gardens, or other features. The mere suggestion of a ceiling and walls—tree limbs overhead or a simple pergola—can also add to the sense of intimacy and enclosure, providing shade and overhead definition to an otherwise open space.

If you must use a wall to gain privacy, build one that uses materials and a design that matches the home and it's surroundings as shown with this adobe wall.

DESIGN GUIDELINES FOR A SUCCESSFUL PATIO
continued

Low built-in benches and a short retaining wall both separate the sitting area of this patio from the rest of the yard. Simple design elements like this can help define the patio's use and give it the feeling of an outdoor room.

ADEQUATE SIZE

Some designers say a patio should be the same size as the interior room that it adjoins. Others suggest it should be one-third the size of the main floor of the house. In any case, the patio should be in proportion to the house and grounds, neither overwhelming nor being overwhelmed by them. It should be the appropriate size for its intended uses and the available space.

How much space is available for the patio? Local setback limits, lot-coverage restrictions, and easements may limit how much of the property can be turned into a patio. Backyard activities, such as gardening or outdoor games, may impose other limits.

How many functions will the patio serve? Perhaps you'd like to eat meals there, as well as soak in a hot tub. Assign different functions to different parts of the patio,

allowing ample space for activities, traffic flow, and outdoor furniture (which tends to be bigger than indoor counterparts). Personal relaxation, for example, may not work well in the same space where children play, and a basketball hoop could be disastrous located too near a dining area.

Where different functions must take place close to each other, planters, trellises, benches, or even a change in paving patterns can help define areas. Structural solutions, such as building a T-shaped patio or building a patio on different levels, work even better—but are often more costly.

EASY, INVITING ACCESS

The main door to the patio should be wide enough to permit easy in-and-out traffic flow as well as provide an inviting view from inside the house. French doors, atrium doors, and sliding doors work especially well because they give a sense of continuity between the indoors and outdoors. If the house does not already have such openings, consider including them in your patio plan and budget.

A patio that's difficult to get to probably won't be used. It's best to site the patio so that you can either step directly onto it from the house or reach it via a path leading directly from the house. Patios adjacent to the house should be close to the level of the house floor. If winter brings snow, set the patio 3 inches lower than the floor to keep snow out of the house. If rain is your main concern, you only need to build the patio about 1 inch lower than the floor. You might want to consider building a ramp at the change in level to permit easy wheelchair access and to prevent toe-stubbing. If the drop to the patio level is greater than 3 or 4 inches, steps might be required. Size the steps as if they were standard stairs (see pages 32-33).

The main function of the patio should be tied to the main function of the adjoining room. If the patio will often be used for meals, it should be close to the kitchen. If the patio will be used for entertaining, it should be accessible from the public rooms of the house. A patio geared to recreational activities is best located off the family room. Make patios that serve more than one function large enough to be accessible from more than one room in the house.

COMFORT AND PLEASURE

A patio should offer more than privacy, protection, and plenty of seating. It should be sited to take advantage of the natural

surroundings—cooling breezes, warming sun, shade trees, subtle garden fragrances, pleasing views, or shrubs that buffer street noises. Even if there isn't a lot of flexibility in locating the patio, there are still ways to work with the environment. Pergolas can filter hot sunlight, and vines growing on them can screen out an unattractive view. Air can be circulated on calm days with a portable fan, and bug lights and bee traps can help control insects.

Comfort also is enhanced by amenities tailored to the needs and interests of the family. They can be as simple as a basketball hoop or complex as a spa. Consider a natural gas grill for an enthusiastic chef, or pocket gardens and a gardening bench for the gardener of the house. A vine-covered colonnade can serve as a transition from active to quiet areas, and a fountain in a shallow pool could inspire peaceful reflection. Add whatever weather-worthy features increase the enjoyment of the patio and fit the budget.

Without the easy access these french doors provide, this brick patio would have been pretty, but used far less. Always consider traffic flow to and from the patio when you design it. It is, after all, another room of the house, it just happens to be outside.

A privacy fence and the dense foliage that hides it give visual privacy and muffle unwanted noise.

DESIGN GUIDELINES FOR A SUCCESSFUL PATIO
continued

Think creatively when confronted with a landscape problem such as the rocks in this patio. Rather than spend the time to remove the rocks, they are incorporated into the patio's very structure, helping it blend in with its surroundings.

VISUAL HARMONY

Achieving visual harmony on a patio requires the skillful blending of many diverse elements, but the two dominant elements are the shape of the patio and the type of material used to pave it. Both give the patio its form, mass, and texture, and define its relationship with the house and yard.

To achieve a sense of unity, the contour of the patio should repeat or blend with the dominant forms of its surroundings. These often are the rectangles of the house, but may also include curves, angles, and free form shapes suggested by property lines, swimming pools, garden beds, or sloping lawns.

The type of paving can radically affect the overall appearance of the patio. Select a paving material that complements the style of your home in the context of the yard and garden. For example, a quarry tile patio might look out of place with a Victorian house, but would be perfect with a Southwestern adobe. The paving material does not necessarily have to match the house's foundation, but it should not conflict with it, either. For example, a flagstone patio next to a concrete foundation will work fine, but next to a red brick foundation it might look discordant.

Select accessories and furnishings that are in harmony with the patio and tie together the house and yard. Fortunately, there is a style of patio furniture to fit almost every taste and budget, from sleek, contemporary pieces to classic cedar or charming, old-fashioned wicker.

SITE GUIDELINES FOR A SUCCESSFUL PATIO

U nless a patio is part of the original plans for a new house, there may be little choice about where it will go. Even so, moving the edges a few feet one way or another can mean catching (or avoiding) the sun, optimizing the microclimate, and allowing access to utilities.

ORIENTATION TO THE SUN

Assuming some degree of flexibility, it is possible to determine, and therefore manipulate, how much sun or shade the patio will get. In the northern hemisphere, the south side of the house receives sun most of the day. In summer the sun is very high in the sky, beating down on the roof. In the winter the sun is quite a bit lower, and hits the wall instead of the roof. A south-facing patio with a lattice-covered pergola would have sun filtered through the pergola in summer, and full sun in winter—a nice arrangement in a warm-cold seasonal climate.

If the south wall of the house is always in the sun, the north wall is always in shade. In the summer when the noonday sun is high in the sky, the shadow cast by the house may not extend very far into the yard. A patio that extends beyond the shadow line would have both shady and sunny areas in the summer. In winter, however, the patio would have to be very far into the yard to catch the sun. This site would work well in a year-round hot climate shade, and also in colder climates where the patio is not likely to be used in the winter, anyway.

The east side receives morning sun and is shady from midmorning on. The west side starts the day in shade but receives hot sun from early afternoon until sunset. If possible, site the patio to get the right amount of light when it will receive the most use.

Many houses are not situated on a true north-south axis, so a patio on one side of the dwelling receives sun and shade patterns from two directions. A patio on the southeast side of a house, for example, receives sun much of the day but escapes the hot late-afternoon sun. But even if a house is situated on a true north-south axis, a patio that wrapped around the corner of the house could take advantage of combined sun-shade patterns.

SUN AND SHADE

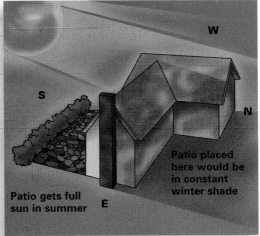

S

W

N

Patio placed here would be in constant winter shade

Patio gets full sun in summer

E

WINTER SUN

Sunlight is perhaps the most predictable factor when considering the site of a patio. Make sure your patio is placed so it receives some of both so you can sit in the sun on cool days and move to a shady area when it's hot.

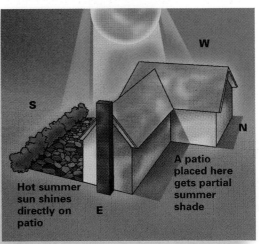

S

W

N

A patio placed here gets partial summer shade

Hot summer sun shines directly on patio

E

SUMMER SUN

SITE GUIDELINES FOR A SUCCESSFUL PATIO
continued

CREATING A MICROCLIMATE

You'll soon discover that the air on your patio feels a little bit different from the air a few feet away. The materials that go into the patio and the arrangement of those materials create what's called a microclimate.

Different paving materials, for example, determine how much heat from the sun is absorbed each day. They also affect how much light is reflected. A light-colored concrete patio reflects a lot of heat. Its surface is comfortably warm, but because it also reflects sunlight, it may seem harsh and glaring. On the other hand, dark brick moderates the harshness of bright sunlight, but absorbs the heat. This makes the patio surface uncomfortable to walk on with bare feet during the day, but the stored heat radiates during the cool evening, prolonging the daytime warmth. A patio placed on top of a hill is warmer on a calm day than one at the base of a hill, because cold air flows downhill. At the base of the hill, cold air can get trapped by retaining walls, fences, or house walls, making a patio there quite cool in the evening.

Wind also influences the microclimate of a patio. A pleasant breeze may bring welcome relief on a hot day, but gusting winds can make it impossible to enjoy the space at all. Judicious hedge planting and fence placement can baffle forceful winds while not blocking out breezes.

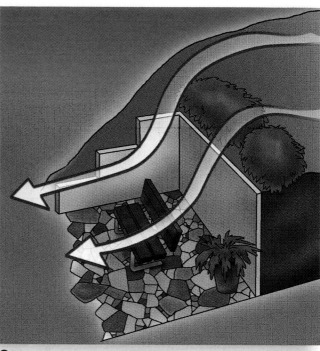

COOL AIR MOVES DOWNHILL

CODES AND UTILITIES

Any patio construction must be in accordance with local building codes and zoning laws. Find out what setback requirements and other zoning regulations need to be considered. Do the neighbors have an interest or a say in what is being planned? Is a scaled site plan or survey required? What are the building codes regarding structures such as fences, walkways, and overheads?

Easements or right-of-ways may restrict your ability to build a patio where originally planned. If, for example, a utility company has a line running through a yard, you might not be able to build any permanent structures, including patios, in that area. It is possible, however, that a mortarless sand-set patio,

which allows quick access to utilities below, would be allowed in areas where a concrete patio is forbidden.

No matter where you build, consider utilities carefully. Verify with the local utility companies where gas, water, sewage, electrical, or communications lines may be. Make sure construction won't cut into them. Make sure you don't pave over areas close to septic tanks or water wells. Avoid underground oil tanks and their openings.

Some patio features require professional plumbing, electrical, or natural gas installations. A spa requires access to running water and a drainpipe. Spas, pond fountains, and waterfall pumps require a ground fault circuit interrupter (GFCI). Lighting systems require electric lines. A natural gas line for a gas grill might be preferable to propane tanks. An exterior phone jack is useful for households that don't want to go cellular. If outdoor activities include watching TV, you'll need an electric outlet and perhaps an exterior cable connection.

Utilities are best run underground to the site—both for safety and to avoid visual clutter. Plot the utility run so that it does not interfere with anything else in the area. Have the systems roughed-in by professionals after excavation, but before you lay any of the foundation.

SUN AND HEAT REFLECTED DURING THE DAY

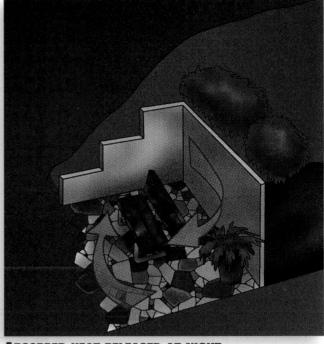

ABSORBED HEAT RELEASED AT NIGHT

TREES, PLANTS, AND THE MICROCLIMATE

Unless you're building a brand new house, your choice of patio sites is limited by what you find on the site: It will either be hilly or flat, sunny or shaded. While you have very little control of the terrain, you can moderate the temperature extremes around your patio by carefully planting trees and shrubs.

Trees can provide shade from sunlight, and can break harsh winds. Deciduous trees—oaks, maples, walnuts, and the like—are quite bushy in the summer, but lose their leaves in the winter. Consider planting them in moderate climates where the patio is in use most of the year. The leaves will provide shade in the summer, but let the warming sun shine through in the colder months.

Bushes can provide privacy without creating the abrupt barrier of a fence or wall. Seen from the yard, the bushes are simply part of the landscape. From the patio, the bushes create a sense of intimacy without isolating the occupants from the surroundings.

No matter where in the country you are, your yard will have prevailing winds. The wind is likely to come from different directions in the summer and winter. Watch to see where the wind comes from, and plant to take advantage of it. In the summer, you'll want to channel the wind toward the patio; in the winter you'll want to block the wind.

Large bushes can direct the view away from eyesores toward more desirable views. They can block the glare from neighboring buildings or even the glare from a lake. Bushes will also block, but not eliminate, noise from the street or neighborhood.

As you design your site keep the variety of trees and bushes to a minimum to unify the design, and don't plant deep-rooted trees or bushes near the house where they can undermine the foundation.

TERRAIN

The terrain of your yard is an important factor in designing your patio. If your house, and future patio, are at the bottom of a slope, think carefully about what will happen when rain water comes down the hill and runs into the patio.

Patios are built so they slope gently away from the house. The typical slope is between $\frac{1}{8}$ and $\frac{1}{4}$ inch per foot. Anything less is likely to flood; anything steeper is uncomfortable.

You may need to consider some corrective grading while you're excavating for the patio. If you have problems with a wet basement, for example, putting a patio on the side that leaks may make the problem worse. If the patio must go there, dig a swallow ditch, called a swale, around the patio to direct water away from it, and the house.

HOW TO ADAPT A PLAN TO YOUR HOUSE

Any patio plan in this book can be adapted by changing the paving material. Choose something that matches the landscape and that you're comfortable working with. You can also alter auxiliary structures such as walls, steps, ponds, and overheads. The overall size or shape of any of these plans also can be modified to fit your site.

CHANGING SIZE AND SHAPE

Most of the patios described in this book measure 18 feet by 30 feet, and are based on a multiple of a 3-foot by 5-foot rectangle. Using multiples of 3 and 5 to size a patio gives it pleasing proportions. To make a patio that is larger or smaller, increase or decrease it proportionately, to 15 by 25, for example, or 21 by 35. If you can't get the exact proportions, try to come as close as possible, both for esthetics and to create an area that's easy to use.

Changes in the perimeter measurements often have a great impact on the overall size and utility of the patio. A small difference in perimeter measurements can mean a big difference in usable surface—and in the amount of material needed to pave it.

Don't make your patio too small. Patios should be no smaller than 12 feet by 20 feet or its equivalent area (240 square feet), unless it is intended for a very limited or highly specialized function. A small patio outside a bedroom might be ideal for eating breakfast or sunbathing. The same size patio would be too small outside the family room where everyone used it.

Although an 18-foot by 30-foot patio may seem large, especially when compared to the size of most indoor rooms, it produces a comfortable amount of outdoor living space. It is large enough to accommodate the broader scope of outdoor activities, and allow several different uses at the same time. It is also big enough to hold outdoor furniture.

SHAPE: Typically, a patio has a rectangular shape, although that is not mandatory. It can be any shape that best fits the house and yard. The easiest variations are based on changes to a basic rectangle. For instance, wrapping a deck around a corner of the house or adding an extension will change the patio from a rectangle to an L. Add a broad walkway, and it becomes a U, Z, or a T. A simple approach to varying the basic rectangle is to think of

each leg of an L-shape, Z-shape, or T-shape as a separate section divided from the others by control joints, permanent forms, or edging.

Even free-form and curved shapes can take their cue from the rectangle. Straight sides can be curved to follow the lines of a landscaping feature such as a creek bed. Corners can either be rounded by a curve, or cut by an angle.

Whatever the shape, functional sections should be a minimum of 240 square feet. A 240-square-foot circle, for example, has a diameter of about 17 feet 6 inches. A patio twice that size has a diameter about of 24 feet 9 inches.

CHANGING FOOTINGS

Local climate and soil conditions affect the depth, style, and need for reinforcement of post and stair footings. Be sure to follow local codes—consult your county or municipal building office.

You may be able to do without conventional footings if you're building a structure on an existing concrete patio. You'll need to be sure of three things: (1) that the slab has a properly constructed base, (2) the structure does not bear a lot of weight, and (3) any overhead is not attached to the house. In these situations, if approved by the local building office, you can mount the posts for the structure in galvanized post anchors fastened directly to the concrete slab. The base of the patio will absorb the shock of soil movement caused by normal freezing and thawing.

For structures built on land that has a lot of fill, it may be necessary to dig exceptionally deep footings and reinforce them with rebar. Filled land settles over time, so stairs and overhead structures attached to a house must be stabilized with footings that reach below the frost line and into undisturbed subsoil.

CALCULATING MATERIALS

If you change one of the patio plans in this book, you'll need to recalculate the materials required. Adjustments for the lumber and fasteners are straightforward. Materials such as crushed rock, gravel, concrete, and sand are sold by volume, however, any changes will require a bit of calculation. Many suppliers can help you calculate your material requirements.

HOW TO MAKE CALCULATIONS

CALCULATING OTHER MATERIALS:
Materials such as reinforcing mesh, pavers, and bricks are sold by the square foot or the equivalent. A 540-square-foot patio needing reinforcing mesh would require 540 square feet of mesh.

Determining how many bricks or pavers are required depends on the size of the materials you select. If, for example, it takes 5 pavers to cover a square foot, multiply the area times 5—540 sq ft × 5 = 2,700 pavers.

If a paver covers more than a square foot, it's simpler to divide the area of the patio by the area covered by the paver. For example, one 18-inch square paver covers 2¼ square feet. Divide the patio area by 2.25, and it looks like this: 540 sq ft ÷ 2.25 = 240 pavers.

AREA: The amounts of the material needed to build a patio is based on the square footage, or area, of the patio. To calculate the area of a square or rectangular patio, multiply the length times width in feet. The formula to calculate the area of a circle is radius squared times pi—first determine the radius, which is half the diameter of the circle; multiply the radius by itself and then by 3.1416. To find the square footage of a triangle with a 90° angle in it, multiply the two shortest sides together and take half (side × side × ½).

To avoid the math, or to estimate the square footage of a complex or an irregular shape, draw the shape on graph paper, with each square representing 1 square foot. Then count all the total and partial squares within the patio to arrive at the approximate total area.

VOLUME: Volume, measured in cubic feet or cubic yards, is based on the thickness of the patio, as well as its surface area. First determine the volume of material in cubic feet. The formula is area in square feet times depth in feet. For example, the area of an 18-foot by 30-foot patio is 540 square feet. The proposed depth of a gravel base is 4 inches. Convert the depth measurement to feet (4 inches equals ⅓ or .3334 foot) and the calculation looks like this—540 sq ft × .3334 ft = 180 cubic feet.

If you need to convert cubic feet to cubic yards, there are 27 cubic feet in a cubic yard (3×3×3=27). The formula for conversion is cubic feet divided by 27. In our example, 180 cubic feet ÷ 27 = 6.67 cubic yards.

Finally, add approximately 10 percent for waste allowance. The formula is cubic yards times 1.10. In this example 6.67 cubic yards × 1.10 = 7.3 cubic yards. Most supply houses don't sell fractions of a cubic yard, so you'll have to round up.

Adjust the final number of bricks or pavers you'll need by 10 percent so that you'll have replacements for any that are misshapen. You may also want to keep a few of the extra around for repairs so you'll have bricks or pavers that match the originals.

BUILDING A PATIO

In designing your patio, you'll not only choose a plan, you'll choose the surface for the patio. The surface you choose influences the way you build your patio more than anything else. You have two broad choices: a patio supported by (or made of) concrete, or a patio supported by a sand base. Either choice will work with any of the patios in this book.

Each surface has advantages. A concrete patio is durable. It makes an excellent base for a mortared brick or stone patio, and it provides enough support to keep it from cracking over time—but it's also a major undertaking.

A sand-base patio, on the other hand, is well-suited to the do-it-yourselfer. A gravel base provides drainage and support for sand which in turn supports the patio's surface. The surface can either be brick or one of the many types of precast concrete pavers that let you create intricate patterns without headaches. You won't be able to use mortar, but sweeping sand between the joints locks the surface together for a firm, stable patio.

Building either type of patio isn't complicated, but it is work that benefits from meticulous attention to detail. This section shows you how to lay out and excavate the site with the proper slope for drainage, how to make a sand-base patio, how to make a concrete patio, and how to use a concrete slab as a base for fieldstone, tile, and other surfaces. It also explains patio steps, anchored posts, and other structures that often are a part of a patio plan.

When calculating the time, effort, and money it will take for you to create your patio, don't forget about the little extras that can make a patio look even more elegant—like this short mortared wall.

LAYING OUT AND EXCAVATING THE SITE

The first step in construction is layout. This begins by outlining the patio with stakes and string. The hole for the patio needs to be larger than the actual patio and the corners don't need to be precisely square. For now, at least, layout can be pretty simple. Drive four 2×2 stakes into the ground 4 inches beyond where the corners of the patio will be. Tie strings between them to mark the edges of the excavation.

Tape shovel to show how deep to dig

Measure down from layout lines to gauge depth of excavation

Excavate the staked enclosure to the approximate depth that will accommodate all the layers of material that will go into the patio. That usually means an excavation about 8 inches deep, but as you'll see, it varies depending on the surface you choose. When excavating a flat piece of ground, you can put pieces of tape on the shovel handle to mark the proper depth.

If you dig too deep in a spot, do not refill and tamp. Just use more base material to fill the low spots. Unexcavated subsoil provides the best support for the base you'll lay on top.

BATTER BOARDS AND STRING LINES

At this point, you need to refine your layout with batter boards and a carefully measured and sloped grid of lines over the patio. Batter boards are horizontal boards used to lay out the patio. They are useful for refining the string placement without having to move the support stakes (see opposite page).

Be sure the stakes nearest the house are at the exact corners of the patio. Make a mark on the stakes at the point level with the finished surface of the patio. Measure up 6 inches and attach mason's line at the marks. (Mason's line won't sag like regular string does.) Drive a nail or make a notch in the stakes to keep the line from sliding down.

Next, build batter boards from three pieces of 1×4, each roughly two feet long. Place the batter boards 1 to 4 feet outside corners of the patio furthest from the house. Stretch line

USING A WATER LEVEL

A water level is a simple way to find two points that are level with each other. It works on the principle that water always seeks its own level. There are two types of water level: A simple colored water level relies on sight readings, and a more costly electronic water level sounds a beep when the level is reached. Both work roughly the same way: A long tube filled with water has either a gauge or beeper on one end, and an indicator on the other. Hold one end at a reference point—a mark on the wall or the top of a batter board, for example. Stretch the tubing to the location you want to mark. Lift the loose end of the tube slowly until the colored water reaches the indicator in the simple gauge, or the beeper sounds in the electronic gauge. Mark the spot—it is at the same level as the reference point.

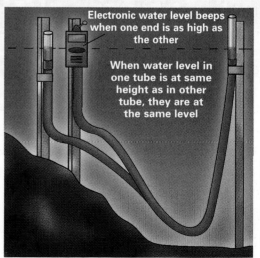

Electronic water level beeps when one end is as high as the other

When water level in one tube is at same height as in other tube, they are at the same level

USING A WATER LEVEL

between batter boards and stakes to mark the rough outline of the patio. Even though you'll slope the line later, it needs to be level now. Attach a line level, or use a water level, and adjust the height of the batter board or stake as needed.

Now make sure the corners of the patio are square, first using the 3-4-5 triangle, and then double checking with the opposite corner method.

THE 3-4-5 TRIANGLE: A corner is square when its two sides and diagonal measure a multiple of 3, 4, and 5 feet: 6-8-10, 9-12-15, and so on. Use the largest multiple possible and use the same one for each measurement. Measure out from the corner along a distance equal to the multiple of 3 feet, and mark the string at that point. Do the same along the other side, using the multiple of 4 feet. Then measure between the two marks. If this diagonal is exactly the multiple of 5 feet, the corner is square. If not, adjust the angle by sliding one of the lines along the batter boards until the measurements are equal. Square all four corners of the patio.

OPPOSITE CORNER METHOD: Measure the diagonals between corners. The corners are square when the two diagonal measurements are equal. Adjust the lines as necessary.

Once you've squared the lines the layout lines will cross at the remaining two corners of your patio. Mark the intersections temporarily by driving a stake in the ground.

ADJUSTING THE SLOPE

In order to drain properly, a patio should slope away from the house at a rate of ¼ inch per foot. Now that the corners are square, it's time to lay out the slope. Go to either of the stakes on the side furthest from the house. Measure down from the string ¼ inch for each foot between the house and the stake and make a mark. Drive the corresponding batter board into the ground until the mason's line is at the same height as the mark. Do the same at the other side of the patio.

Check again for square. The lines now mark the edges and slope of your new patio.

Dig out the excavation until it roughly follows the slope. You can measure down from the lines to gauge the slope at the edges of the patio. Check the interior with a gauge rigged from a 2-foot level shimmed with a ½-inch drill bit, both taped to an 8-foot 2×4.

If the patio calls for a gravel base, use it to fill any low spots in the earth. If gravel is not in the plans, use dry sand—it smooths and compacts easily. Tamp it lightly with a hand tamper.

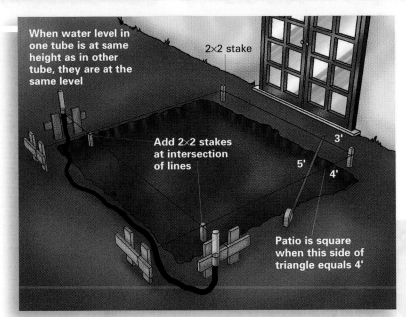

When water level in one tube is at same height as in other tube, they are at the same level

2×2 stake

Add 2×2 stakes at intersection of lines

3'

5'

4'

Patio is square when this side of triangle equals 4'

Patio is square when diagonals are equal and opposite sides are equal length

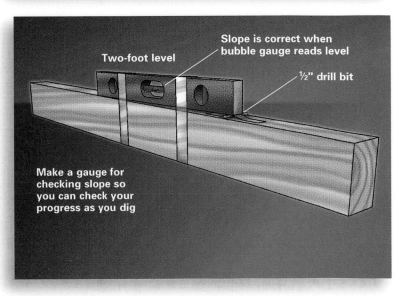

Two-foot level

Slope is correct when bubble gauge reads level

½" drill bit

Make a gauge for checking slope so you can check your progress as you dig

FOUNDATIONS

BRICK IN SAND

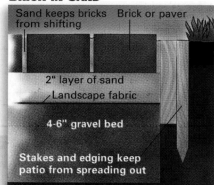

Sand keeps bricks from shifting
Brick or paver
2" layer of sand
Landscape fabric
4-6" gravel bed
Stakes and edging keep patio from spreading out

CONCRETE SLAB

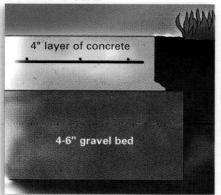

4" layer of concrete
4-6" gravel bed

BRICK IN MORTAR

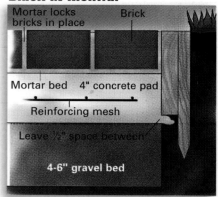

Mortar locks bricks in place
Brick
Mortar bed   4" concrete pad
Reinforcing mesh
Leave ½" space between
4-6" gravel bed

The durability of your patio is dependent, more than anything else on the foundation. There are two basic types of patio construction: sand-base and concrete slab. A sand base is actually a layer of gravel topped by a layer of sand that supports the

WORKING WITH PAVERS

Concrete pavers come in a variety of shapes and colors, and are designed to interlock for a very stable surface with very small joints that appear to be closed. Some pavers are designed to look like bricks, others look like cobblestone, and still others fit together into intricate patterns. Open grass pavers have openings in which you can plant grass, creating a paved areas that looks like a lawn. Pavers with rounded, or chamfered, edges help channel water runoff and prevent chipping during snow removal.

Pavers aren't designed to be mortared. They're designed to sit on a sand bed with sand between the joints. The installation compacts with time and use, so the sand, pavers, and joint sand, interlock with each other. When properly installed, sand-set interlocking pavers are highly stable and durable.

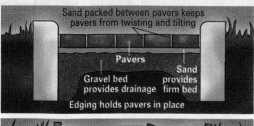

Sand packed between pavers keeps pavers from twisting and tilting
Pavers
Gravel bed provides drainage
Sand provides firm bed
Edging holds pavers in place

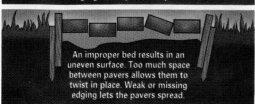

An improper bed results in an uneven surface. Too much space between pavers allows them to twist in place. Weak or missing edging lets the pavers spread.

OCTAGONAL PAVER

OCTAGONAL PAVER PATIO

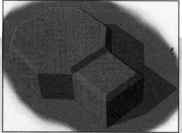

CHAMFERED CONCRETE PAVER

CHAMFERED PAVER PATIO

PLANTABLE PAVER

PLANTABLE PAVER PATIO

MULTIWEAVE CONCRETE PAVER

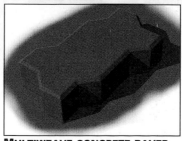

MULTIWEAVE PATIO

surface of the patio. A concrete slab, as its name implies is a solid concrete surface that can be left as is or covered with mortar and then brick, stone, or tile.

SAND BASE

A sand base is usually covered with specially made bricks or concrete pavers. You'll fill the joints between them with sand, which pushes the individual units against a border, and locks the patio place. Don't put mortar in the joints of a sand-bed patio. The sand will shift enough to crack the mortar.

After excavating the site, spread the gravel in layers no more than 4-inches thick on unexcavated subsoil. Tamp, and add more gravel until the base is between 4 inches and 6 inches deep. Your patio will be no stronger than the base beneath it, so pack the gravel well. You can pack the gravel with a hand tamper, but on a patio, it's worthwhile to rent a power compactor.

Sand-base patios need an edging strip thicker than the surface to anchor the patio and keep it from spreading out. Before you add the sand, set the edge of your patio. To position the edging, lay a trial run of brick or pavers along the perimeter of the patio. Trim the edging to fit snugly against the brick or pavers, and then stake it in place.

SAND BASE

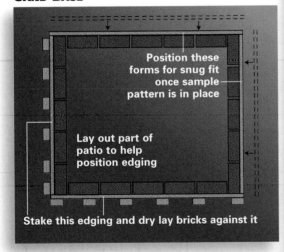
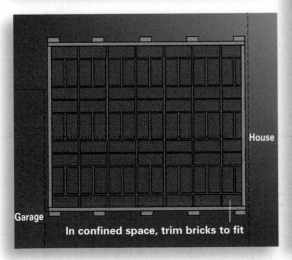

Position these forms for snug fit once sample pattern is in place

Lay out part of patio to help position edging

Stake this edging and dry lay bricks against it

House / Garage / In confined space, trim bricks to fit

BORDER EDGING

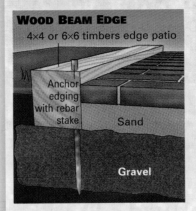 **WOOD BEAM EDGE** — 4×4 or 6×6 timbers edge patio / Anchor edging with rebar stake / Sand / Gravel

 **STAKED WOOD FORM EDGE** — Stake and 1× keep patio in place / Sand / Gravel

 **FLUSH CONCRETE EDGE** — Precast concrete edging holds bricks

 **ANGLED BRICKS** — Set bricks in a concrete bed to keep edging in place

Without edging, the bricks or pavers in a sand-base patio would spread apart. Edging, anchored around the edge of the patio, holds everything in place. Edging can be anything from concrete "bumpers" to decorative beams and bricks. Anchor timbers with lengths of rebar. Anchor wood with stakes attached below grade. Set bricks into concrete trenches deeper than the surrounding excavation, or put commercially available plastic restraints around the edge.

Put the edging in place, and then measure down from your layout lines to make sure it follows the slope of the patio.

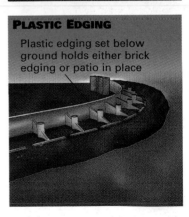 **PLASTIC EDGING** — Plastic edging set below ground holds either brick edging or patio in place

Add or remove dirt, as necessary, to create the proper slope.

FOUNDATIONS
continued

Lay landscape fabric over the gravel to keep the sand from filtering into it and to help block any weed growth. Spread a 2-inch-deep layer of sand over the fabric and rake it smooth. To create the perfectly flat surface you'll need, rest a notched board, called a screed, on the edging and pull it across the sand, as shown. For extra-wide patios, you can set temporary screed guides in the sand.

Starting in one corner of the patio and working outward, carefully lay the bricks or pavers roughly ⅛-inch apart. Keep your weight on the surface you've just laid, and set the bricks or pavers without twisting or sliding them.

When all the bricks or pavers are in place, tamp them with a rubber mallet to set them in place. Use a level and string line to keep the surface even and sloped away from the building.

Once you've set all the bricks, spread a thin layer of sand over the paving and work it into the joints with a stiff broom or brush. Wet down and repeat this process until the joints are packed full—the sand between the bricks forces them against the edging, and helps lock them in place.

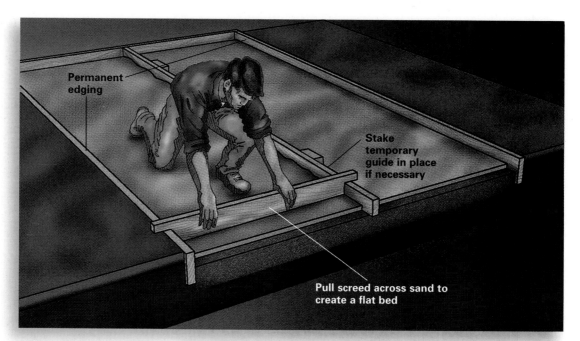

Permanent edging

Stake temporary guide in place if necessary

Pull screed across sand to create a flat bed

GOOD DRAINAGE

■ Make sure you slope the patio bed—as well as the patio—at a rate of ¼ inch per foot. This will keep water from undermining the base and causing the surface to sag.

■ Water drains from the surface of the patio through the sand and then into the gravel bed. Don't ignore the landscape fabric that separates the sand and gravel beds. Without it, the sand will sift down into the gravel, and the patio will sag. Eventually, the sand clogs the gravel, causing the patio to flood in heavy rains.

■ If something does go wrong, a sand-bed patio is easy to repair. Remove the bricks or pavers in the damaged area, and add or screed the sand to make a level bed. Put the paver back in, replacing it if necessary, and sweep sand around the joints.

Lay bricks one row at a time

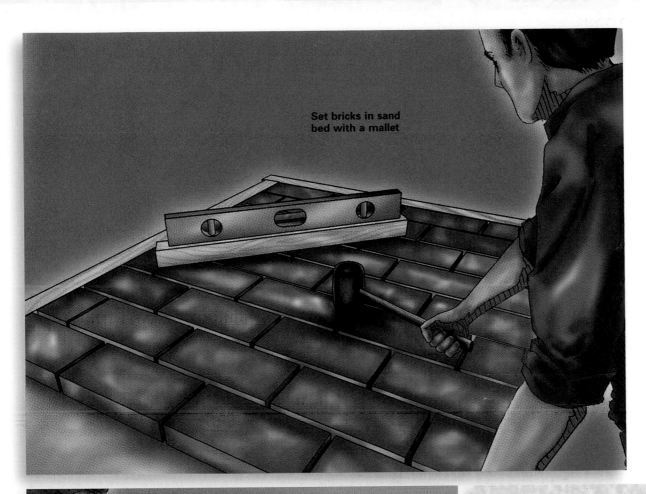

Set bricks in sand bed with a mallet

Sweep sand between bricks to keep them from shifting

A PROPER FOUNDATION

A sand-bed patio is remarkably durable. Paying attention to construction details will help keep it maintenance free:

■ If you don't tamp the gravel well as you install it, it will settle, causing the patio to sag. When you're building the patio, dump the gravel in 4-inch layers. Compact each layer well before you put in the next. It's worth renting a power compactor to speed up the job.

■ Install the edging carefully. It's more than a pretty border. It keeps the patio in place. Without it, the bricks or pavers will spread, and become uneven with use.

FOUNDATIONS
continued

CONCRETE PATIOS

PREPARING FOR THE CONCRETE

■ GRAVEL SUBBASE: Undisturbed subsoil is the best base for a concrete patio. In most areas, however, you also need a layer of gravel to provide drainage. Check to see what's required in your area. If gravel is needed, spread it in layers a maximum of 4-inches thick, tamping and adding to it until the base is 4 inches to 6 inches thick depending on local requirements. You can either tamp it with a power compactor or with a hand tamper, but tamp it well: The concrete will crack if the gravel is packed too loosely.

If you don't need gravel resist the temptation to rake the subsurface smooth. Leave the dirt as it is, hard and well compacted.

CROSS-SECTION OF A CONCRETE PATIO

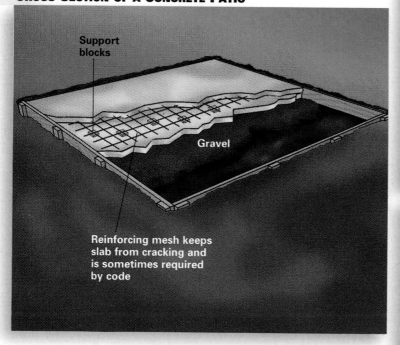

Support blocks

Gravel

Reinforcing mesh keeps slab from cracking and is sometimes required by code

■ ISOLATION JOINTS: Isolation joint strips, also called expansion joint strips, separate the new concrete and any existing concrete structures, such as foundations or driveways. They're strips of treated felt that keep the new concrete from bonding to the old and cracking if the two settle at different rates. Attach the strips to the existing structure with construction adhesive, positioned ¼ inch below the top of the patio.

■ TEMPORARY FORMS: Concrete is poured into temporary forms that give it its shape. They serve a second function as well. After you've poured the concrete, you drag a board across the forms to flatten the concrete and

get it to the right level. Make patio forms with 1×4s raised ½ inch off the gravel or dirt base to create a slab at least 4 inches thick.

Like all patios, a concrete patio should slope the forms away from the house ¼ inch per foot—an 8-foot-wide patio would be 2 inches lower at the edge furthest from the house. Set the forms following the slope of your layout lines carefully. Stake the forms securely with 1×4s, 2×2s, or (best) 2×4s, using duplex nails, which remove easily. Set the stakes no more than 4 feet apart.

Coat forms with form-release agent, available at masonry and concrete suppliers, to make them easier to remove. Don't use

BUILD, STAKE, AND SLOPE PATIO FORMS

Undistrubed ground or gravel, if required

Place forms around edge of pad

Set stakes no more than 4' apart

CURVED FORMS

To make a curved form, kerf a 2-by and bend it to shape. To kerf the board, saw evenly spaced notches part way through the flat side of the board, stopping about ¼ inch before you cut through. Make the cuts with a circular saw, guided by a speed square, or on a table saw or radial arm saw. The more kerfs per inch, the tighter you can bend the board. Bend the lumber so the cuts close—bending further will only snap the board. Support the form with stakes 18 inches to 24 inches apart.

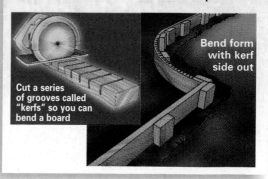

Cut a series of grooves called "kerfs" so you can bend a board

Bend form with kerf side out

crankcase oil, even if it is an old standby. It's a hazardous substance and will leech into your your soil and eventually the water table.

■ REINFORCEMENT: If engineering plans or local codes call for it, you'll need to place wire mesh reinforcement in the slab, to tie it together should it crack. You'll also want mesh if you've covering the slab with pavers or tiles.

Use flat mesh reinforcement sheets for a patio. They should be made of 6-gauge wires that form 6-inch squares, called six-by-six six-six mesh, or more simply 6-6-6-6. Mesh can be cut most easily with light-duty bolt cutters. Brush off dirt and loose rust before using the mesh.

Overlap adjoining sheets of mesh by one square. Although some construction calls for wiring the mesh together, it's not necessary in this application. In order to keep the edges from rusting, leave a gap of 1½ inches between the mesh and the edges of the slab.

Support the mesh in mid-slab by placing it on wire or plastic reinforcement chairs or on commercially available 2-inch concrete blocks made for the job. Don't use brick for support—it soaks up water from the concrete and weakens the mix.

USING MORE CONCRETE TO SAVE MONEY

Depending on the cost of materials in your area, you can sometimes save money and get a stronger slab by increasing its thickness by an inch (from 4 inches to 5 inches) and leaving out the mesh reinforcement.

WORKING WITH THE CONCRETE:

Concrete cures best when the temperature remains between 50° and 70° Fahrenheit over the course of a week. Avoid pouring concrete in extremely hot or cold weather.

Have ready-mix concrete delivered by a truck, unless you cast it in sections with forms that become part of the patio. (See **Courtyard Patio,** page 42). Dry, bagged mix comes in 40-, 60-, and 80-pound bags, and it could literally take hundreds of them to finish the job.

■ CONCRETE SPECIFICATIONS: Air-entrained concrete (concrete with air bubbles in it) is best for most uses. It is mandatory for outdoor use in a freeze-thaw climate—the bubbles help keep the concrete from cracking. For icy climates, entrained air content should be 5 percent to 7½ percent. For mild climates,

around 3 percent air entrainment gives the concrete a nice buttery feel when finishing. It also reduces the water that builds up on the surface, which lets you begin finishing sooner. Entrainment requires power mixing and is best provided by a ready-mix supplier.

Concrete mixtures vary, depending on use. For a patio, you'll want concrete with a maximum-size coarse aggregate (gravel) no larger than ¾ or 1 inch and a slump of 3 inches to 5 inches. (Slump is a measure of concrete's workability.) Specify a minimum 28-day compressive strength of 3,500 psi for mild climates, and 4,000 psi for freezing climates. It may be necessary to increase the cement content to achieve this, but leave this up to the dealer.

If the ready-mix truck will have trouble getting to the patio site, you can have the concrete pumped from the truck. It costs extra, so talk it over with your dealer.

■ PLACING THE CONCRETE: Be ready before the ready-mix truck arrives. To begin with, you'll need a lot of helpers. You'll need at least two workers to place the concrete, and at least two more to begin finishing it. You'll need two more workers with rubber-tire construction wheelbarrows if you need to transport the concrete from the street. If the patio is large, get more help.

Minimum tools include a wheelbarrow, shovel, straightedge, margin or small pointing trowel, bull float, edger, jointing tool, magnesium float, water hose with spray nozzle, and curing materials such as wet sand, plastic sheeting, burlap, or curing compound.

Concrete is caustic. Get safety glasses and leather-palmed work gloves for everyone. Anyone who will wade into the mix—and someone will have to—needs rubber boots.

Before placing any concrete, dampen the subgrade with spray from a garden hose. This keeps the ground from drawing water out of the mix. Spray until the soil is damp, but not puddled.

The stone, cement, and sand that make up concrete can separate if the mix is treated roughly: Use a wheelbarrow with pneumatic tires. Set up ramps supported on blocks so the wheelbarrows can cross over the forms without dislodging them.

Dump the first batch against the forms as close as possible to its final position. Dump each batch against the one before it, so the batches will bond to each other. Don't rake concrete into place—it separates the ingredients. If necessary, use D-handled flat-ended spades to shovel the mix into place. Work the spades up and down along the forms, removing any air pockets against the forms. Fill the forms slightly higher than the top.

FOUNDATIONS
continued

■ FINISHING THE CONCRETE: As one pair of workers fills the forms, the other pair "strikes it off" or "screeds" it. Starting at one end, they pull a long, straight 2×4 across the forms. This removes any excess, and levels the slab with the forms. It also removes high spots and fills in low spots for a smooth, though ridged

Pull screed across wet concrete to level it

surface. Slide the strikeoff back and forth across the tops of the forms with a sawing motion, first tilted slightly forward to cut off the surface. Keep a little concrete ahead of the strikeoff to fill in low spots. Work ahead about 30 inches. Fill any low spots that remain with fresh concrete. Then make a second pass with the strikeoff tilted slightly backward to compress the surface.

Once all the concrete is screeded, float the

Remove high and low spots with initial floating

Bull float

surface immediately to smooth it further. On a patio, you'll use a long handled tool called a bull float, pushing it over the surface with its leading edge slightly raised to it keep from digging in. Pull it back with the blade flat on the surface, cutting off bumps and ridges and filling pockets. Overlap passes by about half the width of the float. Stop when water forms on the surface.

Cut the slab away from its forms about 1 inch below the surface using a margin trowel or small pointing trowel.

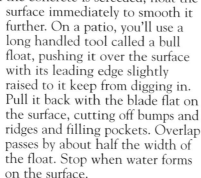

Separate concrete from form with trowel

Give the concrete time to stiffen before further finishing. On hot, dry, windy days, this time can be very short. On cold, damp days, it takes much longer. With air-entrained concrete, little waiting may be needed. In any case, wait until all water has left the surface, there is no water sheen remaining, and you can stand on the surface making no more than a ¼-inch depression.

If the slab is a base for mortared pavers, create a surface the mortar can stick

WORKING THE SURFACE

Don't work concrete if there's water on the surface. Water pulls cement to the surface, weakening it. If water "bleeding" occurs, wait until the water disappears before continuing. With air-entrained concrete, bleeding is seldom a problem.

to by scratching the surface with a folded piece of hardware cloth or metal lath. To reach the far edges of the slab, fasten the wire to a broom handle. Once you're done, cure the concrete as described below.

If the concrete is the final patio surface, start finishing by edging the slab all around the forms and along the isolation joints. The edger is a trowel with a round-over on one side that shapes and compresses the edge of the pad

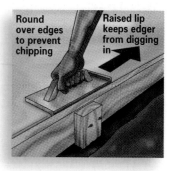

Round over edges to prevent chipping

Raised lip keeps edger from digging in

to prevent chipping. Begin edging as soon as the slab will hold an edge.

Along with edging, or right after it, form control joints. Control joints are grooves cut into the surface. If the concrete settles, the cracks will occur here, rather than down the middle of your patio. (Patios reinforced with mesh, including those that serve as a base for a mortared surface, do not need control joints.)

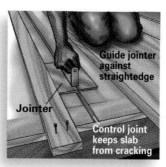

Guide jointer against straightedge

Jointer

Control joint keeps slab from cracking

Use a jointing tool that cuts a quarter of the way through the slab—1 inch in this case. Place control joints to break the patio into slabs no more than 10 feet square and in no case more than 1½ times as long as wide. Guide the jointing tool along a board while moving out across the slab you can kneel on.

After jointing, refloat the surface with a magnesium float. Floating compacts the surface, embeds the gravel, cuts off lumps, fills in holes, smooths out ridges, and removes marks from edging and bull-floating.

Hold the float

A final floating smooths surface

flat on the surface and move it in sweeping arcs, in a slight sawing motion. Magnesium floating alone makes an excellent slip-resistant outdoor finish. Edge and joint the pad again if you like the appearance the tools create. You can stop working the patio surface at this point, or you can apply a specialty surface.

SPECIAL CONCRETE FINISHES

You can work special finishes into the surface of a patio slab before the concrete sets. Include these steps in your overall work and materials plan for pouring a concrete pad.

SALT FINISH: After floating or steel-troweling the concrete, scatter rock salt evenly over the surface (3 to 6 pounds of salt per 100 square feet). Lightly press the salt into the surface so the grains are still

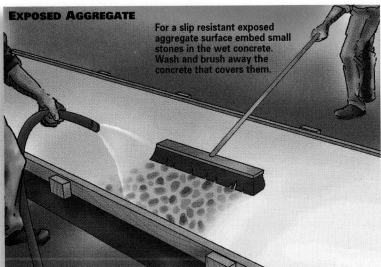

EXPOSED AGGREGATE

For a slip resistant exposed aggregate surface embed small stones in the wet concrete. Wash and brush away the concrete that covers them.

SALT FINISH

Sprinkling the wet concrete with rock salt creates a slip resistant surface

exposed—a section of plastic pipe rolled over the surface works well for this. After the concrete has cured for 7 days, scrub the surface with water and a stiff brush or broom to dissolve the salt. This will leave a pitted surface. Use a salt finish only where there is no winter freezing, since ice in the holes will expand and chip the surface.

EXPOSED AGGREGATE FINISH: After floating the concrete, spread a single, uniform layer of rounded river gravel over the surface. Using a flat board or wooden float, embed the stones flush with the concrete surface. Edge and joint the slab. After the concrete has begun to set, but before it is hard, carefully brush the concrete off the tops of the aggregate with a stiff broom without dislodging the stones. Wash away the loosened material with water. After four days, you can wash the surface with a solution of 1 part muriatic acid to 5 parts water. Add the acid to the water to avoid dangerous spills. Wear rubber gloves, safety goggles, and protective clothing. Rinse the concrete with the mixture, and let the concrete cure three more days. This process normally takes three times longer than regular finishing, so plan either to work small sections at a time in permanent forms, or consult your ready-mix dealer about

adding a retarding agent to the concrete mix for a large slab.

TEXTURED FINISH: You can produce an interesting, skidproof finish by rough troweling the surface with a wooden trowel or float. Move the trowel freely in intersecting arcs over the whole surface.

Another way to texture the finish is by brooming the concrete surface after it has been edged and floated. Wet a stiff-bristled shop broom and shake out the water. Zig-zag it over the surface, or pull it in straight lines at right angles to the flow of traffic. Brooming early in the process makes a rougher texture than brooming later.

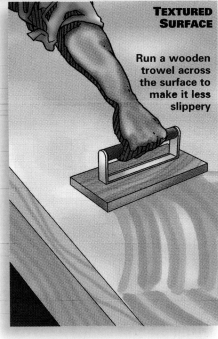

TEXTURED SURFACE

Run a wooden trowel across the surface to make it less slippery

CURING CONCRETE

If concrete dries too quickly, it will be weak and may crack. Keep concrete moist for at least five days in warm weather and seven days in cool weather. You can do this several ways: Keep it damp with a water sprinkler or cover the pad with wet sand, wet burlap, or with plastic sheeting. Be careful with the plastic sheeting: The concrete may cure with a mottled surface if the plastic is in contact with it. If you use burlap, make sure it is clean. You can also use a special spray-on curing compound, but don't use it on a pad for a mortared patio.

MORTARED BRICK AND STONE PATIOS

Mortared brick and stone patios have a concrete base to prevent cracking. The base is a sunken version of the concrete patio described on pages 24-27, reinforced with wire mesh. Make the base as described, positioning it so that the brick, stone, or tile will be an inch or so above grade. Screed the surface, and then scratch it with a rough cloth or metal lath to make the mortar stick better. There's no need for control joints—the mesh reinforcement makes them unnecessary.

Bricks for patios should be type SX where bricks may freeze while wet or MX in milder climates. When you buy bricks, be aware that they have both nominal and actual sizes. Nominal size is the actual size of the brick plus the thickness of a mortar joint. For some brick patterns, you'll need a brick that's twice as long as it is wide. To make sure you're getting a brick that works, tell the dealer how you're using the bricks and what pattern you'll lay them in.

Flagstones come in irregular shapes or smooth-sided rectangles of various thicknesses. Use stones ½ inch to 1 inch thick for patios.

DRY LAYOUT

Make a dry layout of the bricks or stone. Cut and shape them to fit your patio. Aim for a ½-inch joint between stones. Chip off small pieces with a mason's hammer. Large pieces must be scribed and broken off as shown below. Brick joints should be either ⅜ inch or ½ inch, depending on the brick. Ask your dealer.

CUTTING A BRICK

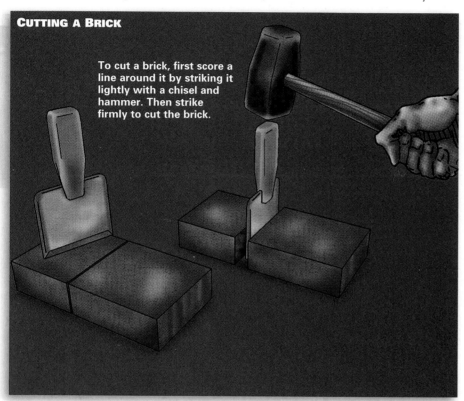

To cut a brick, first score a line around it by striking it lightly with a chisel and hammer. Then strike firmly to cut the brick.

CUTTING A FLAGSTONE

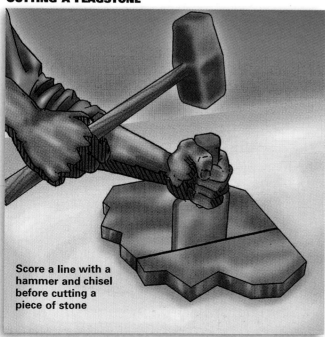

Score a line with a hammer and chisel before cutting a piece of stone

Put the scored line on the edge of a board and strike the stone to cut it

MORTAR BED

Working in small sections, spread layer of Type M mortar over a cured concrete slab. Brick requires a bed ½-inch thick; stone, because it is thicker, should have a 1-inch bed. You can control the thickness of the bed by laying ½ or 1 inch outer diameter pipe on the concrete. Shovel mortar between the pipes, and level it by pulling a board across the pipes. Limit the amount of mortar to an area you can lay in 15 or 20 minutes. Once you know how fast you work, and how quickly the mortar dries, you can adjust the size.

Place the bricks or flagstones in the mortar. After you've laid a few, put a level across them, and check for level. Adjust as needed. Because the bottom of stone is irregular, they need a little extra work at this point. Tilt them up one by one and apply cement "butter" (portland cement mixed with enough water to make a soft butter) underneath. Replace the stones. Smooth, flat bricks don't need to be buttered.

Let the work set for 24 hours, then fill the joints with mortar. The easiest way to do that is to pack all the joints full with a dry mortar mix, made from 1 part cement and 4 parts sand. Brush all the mix off the face of the bricks or stones. Using a very light spray from a garden hose, moisten the joints without washing away the mortar. Continue spraying until joints are completely saturated. Repeat the process if necessary. Keep the paving moist for at least three days to avoid cracking.

BUTTERING A STONE

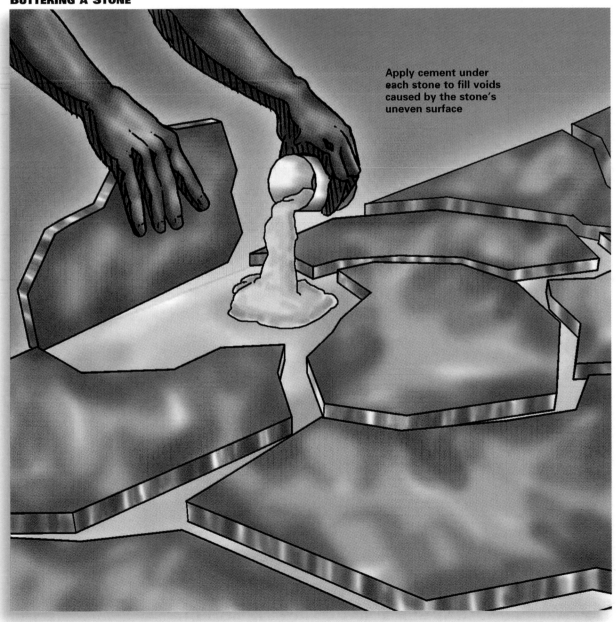

Apply cement under each stone to fill voids caused by the stone's uneven surface

MORTARED BRICK AND STONE PATIOS
continued

WORKING WITH TILE

Tile is an attractive patio surface that comes in numerous types and patterns. Choose tiles that are approved by the manufacturer for outdoor use. They should be low in water absorption, able to withstand freezing and thawing in climates where that occurs, and have a surface that isn't slippery when wet.

Tiles are set in a bed of mortar. For new construction, use the thin-set method, in which you lay either a latex portland cement

LEVELING TILES

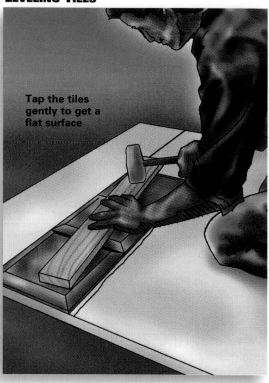

Tap the tiles gently to get a flat surface

MORTAR BED

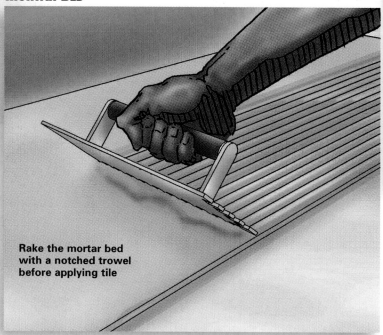

Rake the mortar bed with a notched trowel before applying tile

Level the tiles by placing a piece of wood on them, and tapping gently.

After the tile bed cures overnight, remove the spacers from the joints. Mix commercial tile grout according to manufacturer's instructions. Then moisten the tiles and spread the grout into the joints with a rubber float. After 15 to 20 minutes, wipe the tiles clean with a damp sponge. Allow tiles to dry an additional 30 to 45 minutes. Wipe the tiles off with a soft, dry cloth. If a haze remains, you can lightly "scour" the tiles with a little dry grout mix and a dry cloth. Let the grout cure for at least a week before placing furniture on it.

CUTTING TILES: If you're going to be cutting a lot of tiles on a project, you may want to rent a water-cooled saw, sometimes called a tub saw. If you only have a few cuts, however, you can use hand cutters. There are three types: a simple scoring tool; a pressure clamp that operates like pliers; and a combination scoring and breaking clamp. They all work on the same principle: Score the tile where you want it to break, lay the scored line along an edge or high spot, then apply pressure to either side to snap the tile. Cut irregular shapes by breaking off small bits of tile with a tile nipper.

mortar or dry-set mortar in a very thin bed. Prepare mortar according to manufacturer's instructions. Wet the concrete slab to keep it from absorbing all the water in the mix. Work in small sections at a time, spreading a ¼-inch thick layer of mortar on the slab with the smooth side of the trowel. Then rake back over the mortar with the notched side of the trowel.

SETTING TILE

Press the tiles gently into the mortar

Place the tiles quickly in the mortar bed. Space them with special spacers carried by most masonry suppliers. Press the tiles slightly, but be careful not to force too much mortar up into the joints—you want the joints no more than ⅓ full.

POSTS, PIERS, AND FOOTINGS

Much of the privacy, shade, and ambiance of patios comes from arbors, fences, gazebos, and other structures that use vertical posts. If the structure is to last, the posts need to be firmly anchored to the ground. There are two techniques: You can either bury part of the post in the ground, or fasten it above ground to a concrete pier and footing.

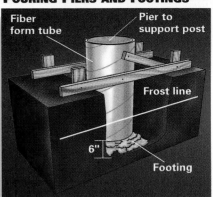

Fiber form tube · Pier to support post · Frost line · 6" · Footing

SINKING A POST

Using a post hole digger, dig a hole that is at least 4 inches larger than the diameter of the post and as deep as half the exposed height of the post. A fence post that stands 6 feet high, for example, needs at least 3 feet buried underground, for a total post length of 9 feet.

In packed soil that is not sandy or overly wet, place 2 inches of gravel on the bottom of the hole for drainage. If the hole is too deep, add more gravel or stones to partially fill it. Set a ground-rated, .40, pressure-treated post in the hole and plumb it as shown in the drawing. Once the post is plumb, fill the hole with 4 inch layers of subsoil, tamping each layer firmly as you go. When you're about a half foot from the top, wedge large stones around the post to keep it locked in place. Finish filling and packing the hole with soil.

If the soil is sandy and loose, very moist, or close to the water table, fill the hole with concrete instead of dirt and rocks. While you can mix and pour wet concrete, prepackaged dry-setting concrete, made especially for post setting, is easier. Put the post in the hole, plumb it, and pour dry mix to within 3 inches to 4 inches from the top. You'll need two 50-pound bags of mix to set a 4×4 post in a 24-inch-deep hole that is 10 inches in diameter. Pour one gallon of water per 50-pound bag into the hole and allow it to soak in. After a half hour, fill the remainder of the hole with soil. Wait at least a half day before placing any stress on the post.

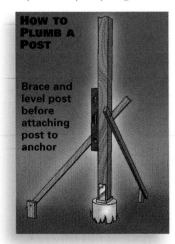

HOW TO PLUMB A POST

Brace and level post before attaching post to anchor

Tamped earth

Add rocks for support

POST BURIED IN SOIL

MOUNTING POSTS ON FOOTINGS AND PIERS

Posts that support an arbor or roof are usually set on piers and footings instead of being buried in the ground. Before digging holes for a footing, check local building codes for the exact size and depth required. Generally, footings should rest on undisturbed subsoil and should reach at least 6 inches below the frost line, if there is one. A post footing should be a minimum of 18 inches in diameter and 6 inches deep. A pier sits on top of the footing and extends 2 inches to 6 inches above the ground. The post sits on the pier and is generally attached by a metal bracket called a post anchor.

The best way to pour footings is as a single unit with the help of a fiber form tube. Dig the hole for the pier and widen it at the bottom for the footing. Pour concrete for the footing. Cut the tube so it will sit on the footing and extend the desired distance above the ground. Level the tube, and while the concrete in the footing is still wet, fill the tube with more concrete. Pull a 2×4 across the top of the tube to strike the concrete level with the top of the form. Sink the base of a post anchor (or a J-bolt for an adjustable post anchor) into the center of the pier at least 2 inches from the edges. Later, when the concrete dries, attach the rest of the anchor, and set and plumb the posts.

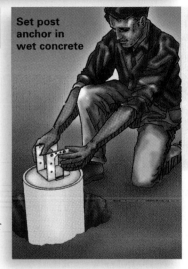

Set post anchor in wet concrete

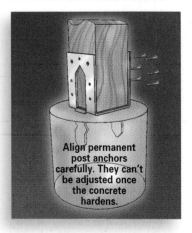

Align permanent post anchors carefully. They can't be adjusted once the concrete hardens.

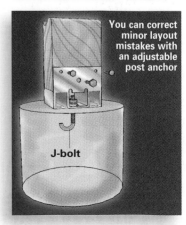

You can correct minor layout mistakes with an adjustable post anchor

J-bolt

CONCRETE PATIO STAIRS

Transitional stairways or steps are sometimes needed in a patio project. A stairway between two patio levels carved into a hillside can lie on a natural slope. Stairs that need to bridge abrupt level changes, such as a patio floor to a doorway in the house, need to be built up from a level surface.

Whether you're building steps into a hillside or against a vertical wall, you need to calculate the total run, the horizontal length from the front edge of the bottom step to the back edge of the top step, not including any landings. You also need to measure the total rise, the distance from the base of the stairway to the top step.

CALCULATING THE RUN AND THE RISE

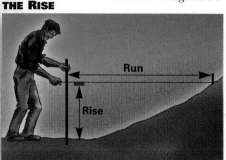

Run

Rise

TREADS AND RISERS

Once you know the total run and rise, plot out a tread and riser to fit the space. For exterior stairways, a rule of thumb is that two risers plus one tread should equal 26 inches.

Treads should be a minimum of 12 inches deep. They also should slope very slightly downward for drainage. To design your forms, draw light right angle steps. Then draw darker lines, angling the risers back 1 inch, and raising the backs of the treads ¼ inch per foot.

SIDE FORMS

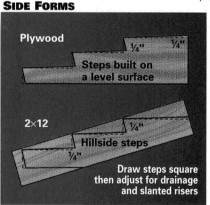

Plywood
¼"   ¼"
Steps built on a level surface

2×12
¼"
Hillside steps
¼"
Draw steps square then adjust for drainage and slanted risers

COMMON SIZES FOR TREADS AND RISERS

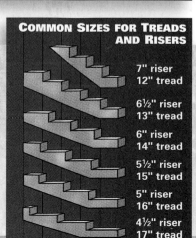

7" riser
12" tread

6½" riser
13" tread

6" riser
14" tread

5½" riser
15" tread

5" riser
16" tread

4½" riser
17" tread

RISERS AND TREADS

To maintain a comfortable stride, there is an inverse relationship between riser height and tread depth—the lower the riser the longer the tread, and the higher the riser the shorter the tread.

Make the front of the form—the part that goes across the riser—from a board with one long edge cut at a 45-degree angle. The beveled edge gives access to the entire step surface during concrete finishing.

STAIR FOOTINGS

A one-or-two-step hillside stair that ties two concrete-slab patios together may not need footings, depending on the soundness of the subsoil and the local code requirements. However, most stairways require at least a footing at the bottom. Flights of more than 3 steps need a footing under the top as well. A concrete step against a house may be able

HILLSIDE STAIR FOOTINGS

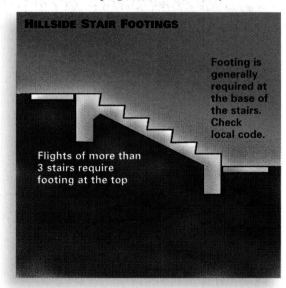

Footing is generally required at the base of the stairs. Check local code.

Flights of more than 3 stairs require footing at the top

to lean against the house's foundation, so that it only requires a footing under the bottom step. Again, check local code requirements. The footings should be at least the width of the tread, extend below the local frost line, and have rebar sticking out the top to tie them to the steps.

HILLSIDE STAIRS: Excavate the site 6 inches below grade and a foot wider and longer than the finished steps. If drainage is poor, excavate an additional 4 inches and add a gravel base. Prop the side forms in place and roughly square them up. Drive 24-inch 2×4 stakes every 2 or 3 feet along one side board. After plumbing the board and checking the slope of the treads (¼-inch drop per foot), fasten the side to the stakes with double-headed nails or drywall screws. Position the other side of the form and stake it in place.

Attach boards to the top and bottom of the side forms, and stake them in place. Place riser boards with the beveled edge facing down and out, and nail them to the side boards.

Brace the center of the risers with a long 2×6 set on edge. Attach it to the risers with 2×4 cleats angled so they won't interfere with the treads. Stake the bottom of this brace firmly. If the stairway is long, stake the top, too.

STAIRS AGAINST A STRUCTURE:

Excavate the site 6 inches below grade and a foot wider and longer than the finished steps. If drainage is poor, excavate an additional 4 inches and add a gravel base.

Before setting it in place, assemble the form by attaching the risers to the sides. Do not put a back on this form. Set the form against the wall. Square and plumb the form, making sure it is level from side to side, and that there is a ¼-inch drop per foot on the treads and the landing.

There will be tremendous pressure on this form from the weight of the concrete. Stake it all around with 2×4s attached with two-headed nails, and brace the stakes. The bigger and taller the stairway, the greater the number of stakes and braces. Make sure there is no space where the form meets the wall. Use silicone caulk or isolation joint material to help close small gaps.

Brace the center of the risers with a 2×4 or 2×6 set on edge and attached to the risers with angled 2×4 cleats. Firmly stake the bottom of this brace.

Paint the wall inside the form with mastic to serve as an isolation joint.

POURING CONCRETE:
Coat the forms with a release agent. Fill the centers with masonry rubble and gravel to reduce the volume of concrete required, keeping the fill well away from the edges and top. Order concrete to be delivered by a ready-mix truck. Spade it around the edges first and then fill the center, working from the bottom step toward the top. Screed the concrete off the treads, smooth with a float, broom-texture the surface, and finish with an edging tool.

Moist cure the concrete in the forms for 3 to 5 days. Then carefully remove the forms and keep the concrete moist for several more days. Steps can be used after the first week.

PLAN AHEAD

Once the concrete is poured, there is no access to the inside of the forms for removing stakes or fasteners. Put all stakes, boards, and nail heads on the outside of the form.

HILLSIDE STAIR FRAMEWORK

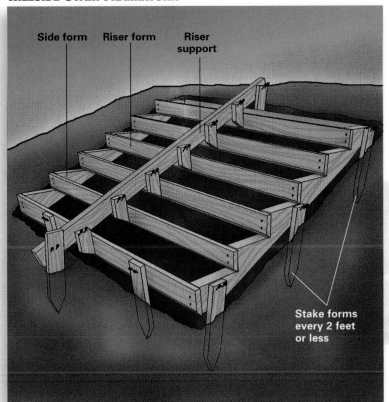

Side form   Riser form   Riser support

Stake forms every 2 feet or less

CONCRETE STEP FORM

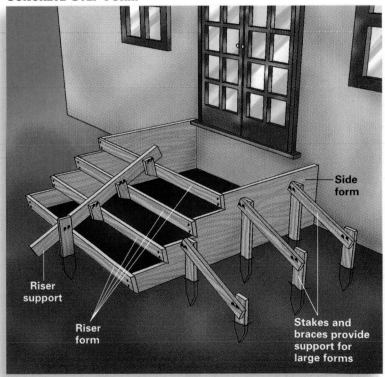

Side form

Riser support

Riser form

Stakes and braces provide support for large forms

Don't try to force a patio design on a specific site. Here, a deck was used to provide a floor-level outdoor sitting area. The patio augments the deck. When you choose a plan or parts of a plan from this book, make sure they fit with the site you've chosen.

PATIO PLANS

This chapter features plans for 14 patios. Each plan is complete and ready to build, including a list of materials required for the project. General patio construction techniques are provided in the preceding chapter of this book, but specific applications and variations are given with each patio plan as needed. Complete directions for building benches, overheads, and even a reflecting pool are supplied too, so you'll be able to achieve the look you want.

The plans cover a range of styles. They include simple walk-out patios that function as an extension of an interior room as well as more complex walk-out patios built on two levels in order to take advantage of a natural slope in the yard. There are detached patios located away from the house. Some of the patios combine the best features of attached and detached patios: part of the patio is close to the conveniences of the house, and the other part provides access to a desirable place away from the house. These are linked by walkways that tie the patio together both functionally and aesthetically.

Even if you are drawn to a particular patio as you leaf through this section, it's a good idea to read all the plans before making a final decision. You may find that a combination of features from different plans might best suit your specific location. (See **How to Adapt a Plan to Your House** on pages 14-15.)

SIMPLE WALK-OUT PATIO

This basic, ground-level patio is easy to construct, and its simplicity makes it adaptable to any size yard, any style house, and most patio budgets. It can serve as the basis for more complex plans that include overheads, planters, or other features.

A one-level concrete slab, located directly outside the room that it serves, creates a simple transition between the indoors and the outdoors. Its proximity to the indoors and the fact that it has no raised edges to trip over—or to interfere with the lawn mower—account for much of its popularity.

Based on an 18-foot by 30-foot rectangle, the patio's leading edges are curved to create an interesting line and make it flow into the surrounding yard. Slight, shallow curves can mimic plantings in the yard some distance away, while tight, looped curves can create

pockets for flowers and shrubs right next to the patio. The basic design is so versatile that its dimensions and materials can be adapted easily to individual situations.

BUILDING THE PATIO

Set the corner stakes for an 18-foot by 30-foot rectangular patio. Then, with a garden hose or a stiff rope, establish the curved edges inside or outside the perimeter. Transfer the curves to the ground with powdered chalk, then remove the hose.

To calculate the correct depth for excavation, first determine the type of base. The most stable base is undisturbed earth. If, however, drainage is poor or the soil is unstable, start with a 4- to 6-inch-deep base of compacted crushed rock, gravel, or pea

TOP VIEW

gravel to provide underground drainage and to help cushion the surface against the effects of freezing and thawing. The exact depth of the base depends on how expansive and wet the soil is—check with the local building department. The finished depth of the excavation is the thickness of the base plus 4 inches of concrete.

Drainage is another factor that must be taken into account when excavating. A patio should slope away from the house at a rate of ¼ inch per foot—and so should the floor of the excavation. Lower the layout lines to follow the slope, and measure down from them to gauge the slope of the hole you're digging.

Build 2×4 forms and stake the straight edges of the patio. For more information, see the pages on building a slab foundation (pages 20-27).

Make concrete forms that follow the curves from tempered hardboard ripped into 3½-inch strips. Drive stakes along the layout line at intervals or 2 feet or less. Bend the hardboard along the stakes, and screw it in place. For more information, see the instructions in **Curved Forms** on page 24.

To keep the pad from cracking, cut control joints in the slab after an initial floating. Cut control joints in both directions, creating squares with 6-foot to 20-foot sides. If you're planning on surfacing the pad with mortar and brick or stone, don't cut control joints. Prevent cracking by putting a layer of reinforcing mesh in the forms before pouring the concrete.

MATERIALS LIST

Element	Quantity*	Material/Size
PATIO		
	10 cu yd	crushed rock or pea gravel
	540 sq ft	reinforcing mesh 6-6-10-10
	30'	expansion joint
	7 cu yd (varies)	ready-mixed concrete

All quantities may vary with site conditions.

FLAGSTONE PATIO WITH PERGOLA

This patio, like the one in Plan 1, is a simple walk-out patio, except that it is paved with flagstones and is shaded with a pergola. The different surfaces of these two plans show how much the paving material affects the look and ambiance of a simple patio.

Although a flagstone patio has a more interesting surface texture than plain concrete, it is more labor-intensive, time-consuming, and costly to install. The stones are supported by a reinforced concrete foundation. Once you've laid the foundation (see pages 24-30) trim the stones to fit before laying a mortar bed and setting the stones.

The pergola is integral to this patio. Carefully plan the patio and the pergola as a unit before beginning construction. Size the roof so that it covers the door between the house and patio, and projects over at least one-third the surface of the patio. See **Site Guidelines for a Successful Patio** on page 11 for the help in controlling the degree of shade. Once you've picked the size and location of the pergola, pour the footings for it before you pour the concrete patio base.

BUILDING THE PATIO

Stake an 18-foot by 30-foot area for the patio. Excavate deep enough to handle all the layers of the finished patio: a 4- to 6-inch gravel subbase, if used; a 4-inch thick concrete slab; a ½-inch thick mortar bed; and ½ to 1-inch thick flagstones. Refer to **Laying Out and Excavating the Site** on pages 18-19 for techniques.

After excavating, and before putting down the patio base, build concrete piers and footings for the pergola posts. Start by marking the exact locations of the posts on the ground. Make the footings at least 18 inches in diameter and 6 inches deep, or the depth recommended by local codes. Pour piers in fiber form tubes with an 8-inch to 10-inch diameter and set post anchors in the wet concrete. Install flexible expansion joint material around the base of the piers.

Now you can go to work on the patio itself. Stake temporary forms around the edge; set reinforcing mesh supports that will place the mesh in the middle of a 4-inch thick slab, as explained on pages 24-26. The mesh prevents cracking, so there is no need for control joints, which could actually cause the patio to crack.

MATERIALS LIST

Element	Quantity*	Material	Length
18'×30' PATIO: FLAGSTONES WITH PERGOLA			
	10 cu yd	crushed rock or pea gravel	
	30'	expansion joint	
	540 sq ft	reinforcing mesh 6-6-10-10	
	7 cu yd (varies)	ready-mixed concrete	
	540 sq ft	paving flagstone, irregular shapes, 2" thick	
9'×12' PERGOLA			
Framing*			
Posts	2	4×4s	10'
Built-up beams	2	2×6s	16'
Ledger	1	2×6	16'
Rafters	17	2×4s	10'
Knee Braces	2	2×6s	8'
Fasteners			
	2	galvanized post anchors	
	15	galvanized joist hangers	
	19	⅜×6" lag screws, washers	
	4	½×6" carriage bolts, washers, nuts	
	2 lbs	16d hot-dipped galvanized joist-hanger nails	
	1 lb	8d hot-dipped galvanized common nails	

*All quantities may vary with site conditions.

***Use rot/insect-resistant lumber.

TOP VIEW

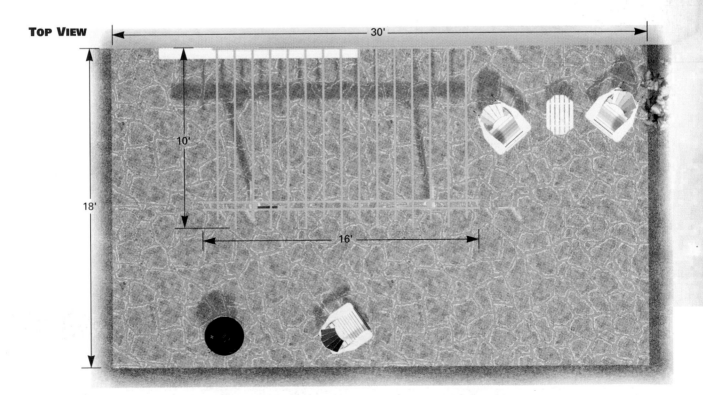

FLAGSTONE PATIO WITH PERGOLA
continued

FLAGSTONES: Make a dry layout of the flagstones. Fit them together with joints that are as close as possible to ½ inch wide. Trim and cut the stones as necessary. Set the stones aside; build forms for the mortar bed, and lay a small section of mortar on the pad. Pull a board across the forms to level it. Set the stones in place, level them, and then paint the underside with a cement slurry as described in **Mortared Brick and Stone Patios** on page 28. Once the first section is in place, move on to the next section of the patio.

Let the work set for 24 hours, then fill the joints with a dry mortar made from 1 part cement and 4 parts sand. Pack the mortar between the stones, and wet them with a very light spray from a garden hose. Moisten the joints without washing away the mortar. Continue spraying until joints are completely saturated. Keep the paving moist for at least three days to avoid cracking.

BUILDING THE PERGOLA

Like any outdoor structure, this one should be built with rot/insect-resistant lumber such as heart redwood, cedar, cypress, or pressure-treated lumber. If you use pressure-treated wood, cutting it will expose wood that has not been treated. Coat the cut surfaces with a preservative.

LEDGER: The pergola roof is supported on one end by posts and a beam. The other end is nailed to a ledger bolted to the house framing. Find the studs in the wall, and position the bolts to go into them. The **Ledger Detail,** below, shows how the ledger is attached to a one story house. On a two-story house, determine the level of the second floor, measure down 2½ inches and draw a level line on the house. Align the top of the 2×6-inch ledger with this line and fasten the ledger through the siding into the framing with ½-inch by 6-inch lag screws. Use washers or other spacers to create a ½-inch gap between the ledger board and the house siding. This gap will prevent moisture from becoming trapped behind the ledger, which would cause the siding to rot.

LEDGER DETAIL

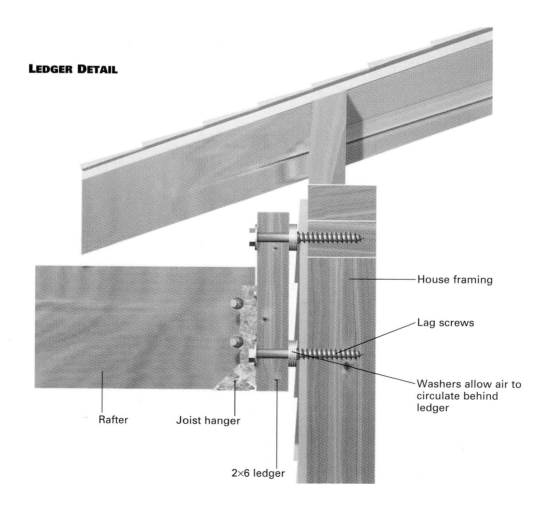

House framing

Lag screws

Washers allow air to circulate behind ledger

Rafter   Joist hanger

2×6 ledger

POSTS: Set the posts in the post anchors, but do not attach them yet. Plumb them with a level, and brace them in place. Mark all the posts at the same height as the bottom of the ledger using a water lever or a line level and mason's line. Take the posts down, cut them, then set them in place again. Plumb the posts, temporarily brace them, and then fasten them to the post anchors.

BEAMS: Attach the 2×6 beams to the posts with ½-inch by 6-inch carriage bolts, positioning the tops of the beams flush with the tops of the posts. Stabilize the structure with 2×6 knee braces connecting each post to the beams as shown below.

RAFTERS: Starting at one end of the ledger, lay out rafters every 12 inches. Nail joist hangers to the ledger at these marks. Cut half of the rafters to extend 12 inches beyond the beam; cut the remaining rafters 6 inches beyond the beam. If you wish, you can shape the outside ends of the rafters with an angle or a decorative curve. Set the rafters in the hangers and nail them in place with hanger nails driven through the hardware.

Attach joists to the beam with hurricane/seismic anchors, which make simple work of the job, in addition to providing extra support.

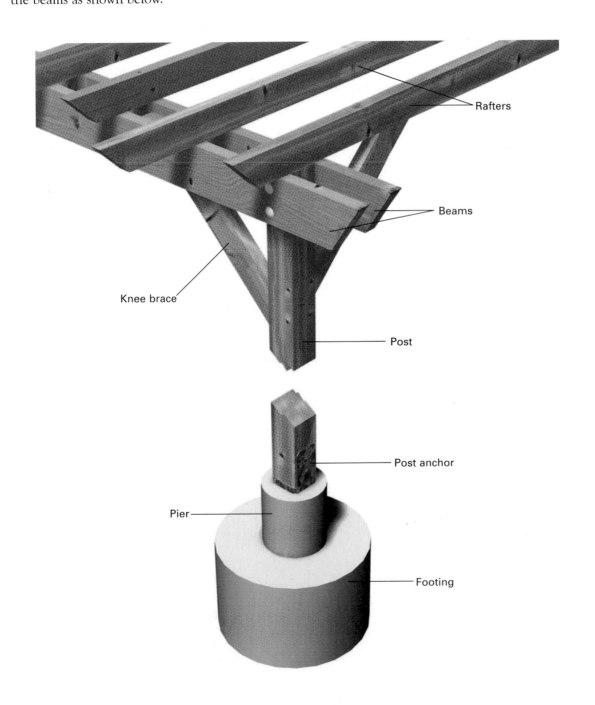

Rafters

Beams

Knee brace

Post

Post anchor

Pier

Footing

COURTYARD PATIO WITH ARBOR

When you build this project, people will notice the arbor long before they realize you've put in a patio, too. Without a doubt, the arbor dominates the design. But taken one step at a time, building the arbor is a manageable job. The footings come first, and are poured before the rest of the patio, as in the **Flagstone Patio with Pergola** on pages 38-41. Once the footings are dry, you attach the posts, plumbing and bracing them carefully. The rest of the job is a matter of nailing beams to the posts, joists to the beams, and rafters to the joists.

An arbor like this works well on almost any patio and you may want to put it on any of the other patios in this book. It's an excellent way to provide relief from the bright sun. On patios that get a lot of direct sun, the arbor provides shade, but is still open to the sky. You can increase the shade by placing the rafters closer together. Planting vines to cover the top provides even more shade.

Because the arbor is freestanding, there's no complicated connection between the house (or roof) and the arbor. The arbor rests in footings that are independent of the rest of the patio. If the footing shifts, it can do so without cracking the rest of the patio. The patio surface is a poured concrete slab with forms that are left in place as decorative wood edging. Dividers that run through the patio are also part of the form work, and divide the job into manageable sections. Pour and finish one square at a time. Each square is relatively small, so you'll probably have to mix your own concrete from bags, instead of buying it from a truck. But instead of having to float, refloat, trowel, and sweep 540 square feet before the concrete dries, you'll only have to handle about 36 square feet at a time. Make the arbor and the forms from the same wood

TOP VIEW

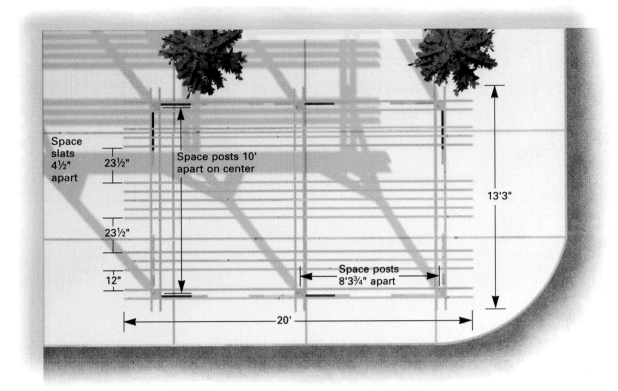

Space slats 4½" apart

23½"

23½"

12"

Space posts 10' apart on center

Space posts 8'3¾" apart

13'3"

20'

to tie the two together visually. Concrete will stain the wood, so protect it by applying finish to the forms before you pour.

BUILDING THE PATIO

Stake out a rectangular 18-foot by 30-foot area for the patio, ignoring the curve for now. Then lay out the interior dividers, creating 6-foot by 6-foot squares. (You can also lay out 6-foot by 10-foot squares or the 6-foot by 7½-foot squares, shown here, but it will make layout of the curve more difficult.)

To lay out the curve, drive a stake at the point nearest the curve where two dividers meet. (If you're using squares larger than 6×6, lay out a 6-foot by 6-foot square in the curved corner, and drive a stake at the corner opposite the curve.) Tie one end of a rope to the stake. Tie a bottle of powered chalk to the rope so that it's 6 feet away from the stake. To draw the curve, pull the rope tight, and pull it in an arc around the stake while squeezing the chalk bottle. The resulting chalk line marks the curved corner of the patio.

After excavating, but before putting down the patio base, build concrete piers and footings for the arbor posts. Start by marking the exact locations of the posts. Dig for footings at least 18 inches in diameter and 6 inches deep, or as required by local codes.

MATERIALS LIST

Element	Quantity	Material	Length
18'×30' PATIO: COURTYARD WITH ARBOR			
	10 cu yd	crushed rock or class 5 gravel	
	540 sq ft	reinforcing mesh 6-6-10-10	
	30'	expansion joint	
	2#	16d hot-dipped galvanized common nails	
	7 cu yd (varies)	ready-mixed concrete	
14'×20' ARBOR			
Framing**			
Posts	6	6×6s	10'
Built-up beams	4	2×8s	20'
Rafters	6	2×6s	14'
Slats	11	2×4s	20'
Fasteners			
	6	galvanized post anchors	
	24	½×10" carriage bolts, nuts, washers	
	10 lbs	16d HDG common nails	

*All quantities may vary with site conditions.

**Use rot/insect-resistant lumber.

COURTYARD PATIO WITH ARBOR
continued

PATIO AND FORMS

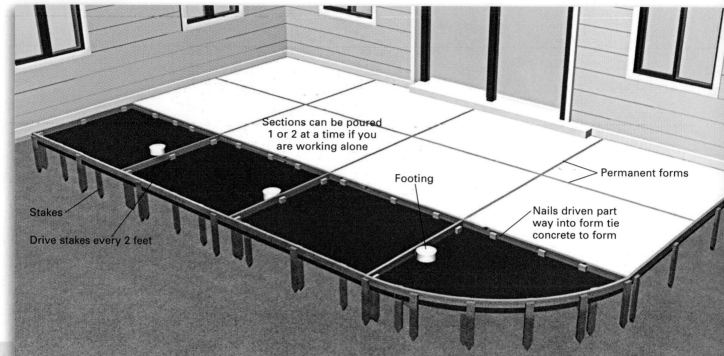

Sections can be poured 1 or 2 at a time if you are working alone

Footing

Permanent forms

Stakes

Drive stakes every 2 feet

Nails driven part way into form tie concrete to form

Place and brace 8 to 10-inch diameter fiber form tube in the holes for the piers. Pour the footing and pier at the same time, placing post anchors in the wet concrete of the piers. Make sure that the anchors are level and plumb and correctly aligned. When the concrete has hardened, wrap flexible expansion joint material around the base of the piers.

Undisturbed subsoil makes the best base for a concrete pad, but soil conditions in many areas require a 4-inch to 6-inch gravel base for drainage. Excavate for a 4-inch thick concrete slab, and a base, if necessary. The quality of the job will depend on the quality of the base. If the base is subsoil, it should be undisturbed subsoil. It's better to have an uneven base than to have a level base made of different density soils, so don't fill in any irregularities with loose soil. A gravel base, on the other hand, must be tightly compacted or the patio will crack. Pour in the gravel in layers no more than 4 inches thick, and compact each layer thoroughly before adding more gravel. Hand tampers, available at most home-improvement centers and hardware stores are fine for the job, but given the size of the patio, it's a good idea to rent a power compactor.

Once the gravel is in place, lay out the forms around the patio as you would for any concrete patio. Because these forms will stay in the ground as part of the patio, be sure to

choose an appropriate wood: Use ground-rated, pressure-treated lumber or heart redwood, cedar, or cypress. Apply a finish to keep the concrete from staining the wood.

When you install the perimeter forms, drive the stakes every two feet. Drive the stakes below the tops of the form so you can bury and plant over them later. Set the divider lumber on edge, following the layout lines you strung earlier. It's best if you join shorter pieces together only where two dividers intersect, but it's best not to have more than one joint at a given intersection. Toenail the dividers together.

Partially drive 16d hot-dipped galvanized nails through the sides of the dividers at 16-inch intervals. These will tie the concrete and the dividers together, keeping the concrete on the same plane with the forms as they settle.

Settling is also an issue wherever the patio meets an existing structure, like a house or driveway. The patio and the structures are likely to settle at different rates, causing the patio to crack. Isolate the patio from existing structures by placing ½-inch wide by 4-inches high expansion joints between them.

Whether you mix and pour the concrete in small sections, or have the ready-mix truck deliver it all at once, take care to protect the forms. A wheelbarrow full of concrete can knock them out of alignment, and when you screed along the forms, it will create an uneven surface.

CORNER DETAIL

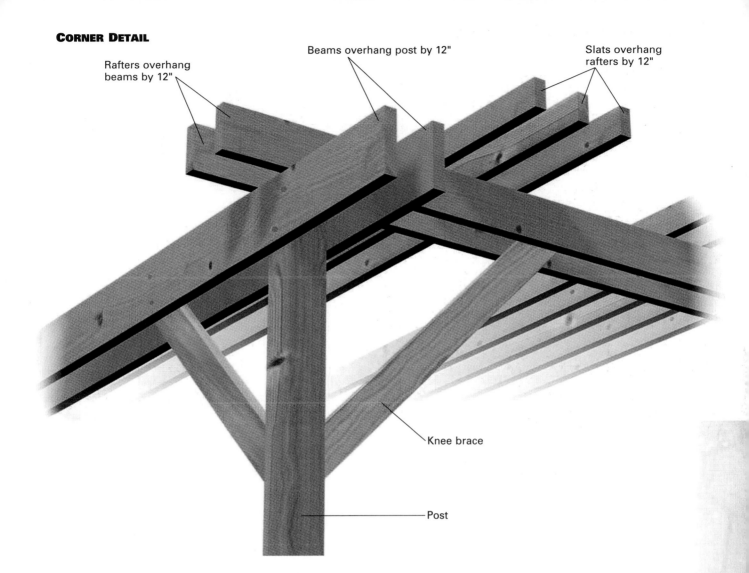

Rafters overhang beams by 12"

Beams overhang post by 12"

Slats overhang rafters by 12"

Knee brace

Post

BUILDING THE ARBOR

This freestanding 14-foot by 20-foot arbor avoids the complicated construction required to cut into and alter the existing roof structure of the house. It also avoids the need to fasten the ledgers to the exterior walls with lag screws. Center the arbor over the patio and build it with 6×6 posts. If desired, face the posts on two sides with 1-by lumber. Use 2×8 beams, 2×6 rafters, and 2×4 slats of rot/insect-resistant lumber.

POSTS: Set the posts in the post anchors, but do not fasten them yet. Plumb the posts and hold them in place with temporary bracing (see **How to Plumb a Post** on page 31). Using a water level or a line level and mason's line, mark all the posts at the same height—8 feet 6 inches above the patio. Take the posts down, cut them, then set them in place again. Plumb the posts, temporarily brace them, and then fasten them to the post anchors.

BEAMS AND RAFTERS: Cut the beams to extend 12 inches beyond the posts on each side. Align the tops of the beams 5 inches below the tops of the posts, and attach them to both sides of the posts with ½-inch by 10-inch carriage bolts, nuts, and washers.

Cut the rafters to extend 12 inches beyond the beams. Set the rafters atop the beams so that they sandwich the posts, then bolt them to the posts with ½-inch by 10-inch carriage bolts. To stabilize the framework, attach 2×6 knee braces between the posts and beams at a 45-degree angle to the posts. Fasten the braces to the beams with ⅜-inch carriage bolts and to the posts with ⅜-inch lag screws.

SLATS: Cut the 2×4 slats to extend 12 inches beyond the rafters. Attach them to the rafters with hurricane/seismic anchors.

FINISH: Finish the arbor with a clear sealer, a wood stain followed by a clear sealer, or a semitransparent stain, as desired. If you prefer, you can finish the arbor with a coat of primer and one or two coats of latex or alkyd exterior paint.

BRICK PATIO

Sometimes, it pays to divide a patio into separate living spaces. A low, flat expanse of even the finest paving material can look formless, and feel uncomfortable, if there aren't any visual clues as to how to use the space. Two simple features help organize this patio into comfortable spaces. The raised dining platform visually divides the patio into eating spaces and living spaces. The platform's location near the doors makes it convenient to the kitchen, and creates a corridor between the doors and platform. The areas on either side of the corridor become their own outdoor "rooms." The smaller area focuses on the yard. The larger area focuses on a second unique feature of this patio—a tree that provides shade and a sense of shelter at the far end of the patio.

The patio measures 12×45 feet—a long, narrow expanse that still provides the 540 square feet typical of the patios in this book. The exaggerated shape of this patio may seem extreme, but it's ideal for certain situations: for small backyards, for backyards with large gardens, or for integrating extremely long houses with the yard. With adaptation, this patio would also work well in a narrow side yard.

The entire patio, including the platform, is a sand-set: A gravel drainage base supports a sand bed, on which you lay the bricks. Finer sand, swept between the bricks packs them tightly against a timber border. This locks the surface together, creating a durable patio that requires neither mortar nor concrete. The 45-degree herringbone brick pattern does require a lot of cutting, however. It's worth your while to rent a water-cooled masonry saw.

TOP VIEW

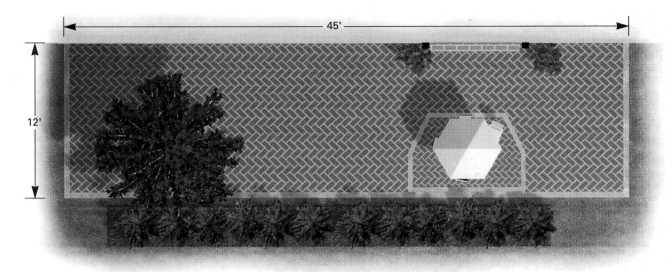

BUILDING THE PATIO

Lay out a 12×45-foot area for the patio. Excavate the patio area deep enough to handle a 4-inch to 6-inch gravel drainage bed, a 2-inch thick sand setting bed, plus the thickness of the bricks or pavers. If you're excavating around an existing tree, be careful around tree roots. Stake a rectangular or square area around the tree that is well back from the exposed roots, and do not excavate inside that zone. If a tree is to be planted after the patio is finished, grade the entire patio surface, and fill in the tree pocket with good dirt when you plant the tree.

This patio begins with the raised dining platform. Build a frame around the edges with 6×6 pressure-treated timbers rated for ground contact. Cut and install the lower layer of timers. Cut and position the top level so the timbers at the 90-degree corners overlap the joints below.

Bore holes through the timbers and stake them with #6 (¾ inch) rebar long enough to reach at least 2 feet into undisturbed ground. In the corners with overlapping joints, put one stake through the center of the overlap. Stake the other corners on each side of the joint.

MATERIALS LIST

Element	Quantity*	Material	Length
12'×45' PATIO: BRICK PATIO			
	12 cu yd	crushed rock or pea gravel	
	5 cu yd	sand	
Paving Brick	2,700	4×8×2¼" bricks	
Edging			
Tree well	1	6×6	12'
	2	6×6s	10'
	4	6×6s	8'
Patio	2	6×6s	12'
	9	6×6s	10'

All quantities may vary with site conditions.

Fill the center of the dining platform with gravel, tamping 4-inch layers at a time, until it is 4 inches below the top of the timbers. Stop for now—you'll add the sand and bricks when you're doing the same for the rest of the patio.

BRICK PATIO
continued

DINING PLATFORM

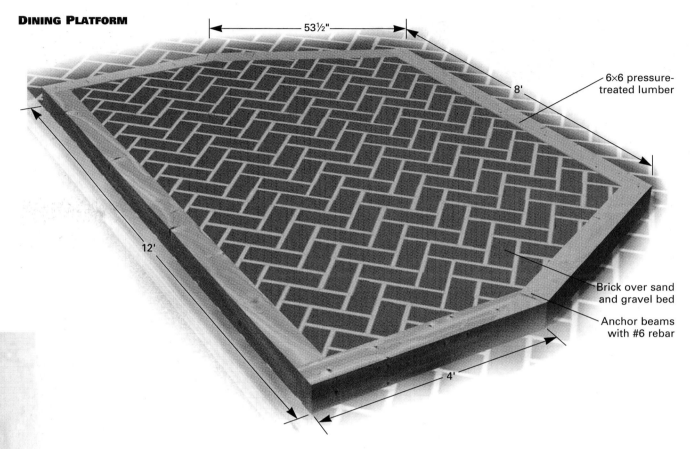

53½"

8'

6×6 pressure-treated lumber

12'

Brick over sand and gravel bed

Anchor beams with #6 rebar

4'

With the dining platform in place, stake 6×6 timbers around the edge of the patio. Place a temporary 2-by edging around the tree opening. Place and tamp a gravel bed, and set a 2-inch sand base on top of it and in the dining platform. See **Sand Base**, pages 21-23, for more information. Lay out a herringbone pattern as described in **Laying a Herringbone Brick Pattern** on the next page.

When a course of bricks gets close to the temporary forms around the tree, replace the forms with permanent 6×6 timber edging. Position the timbers to fit snugly against the bricks—saving yourself a lot of brick-cutting and fitting pieces. Stake the timbers to the ground with rebar.

PATIO CROSS SECTION

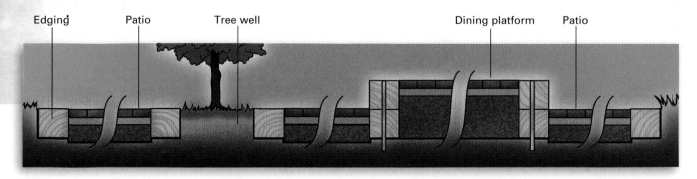

Edging   Patio   Tree well   Dining platform   Patio

LAYING A HERRINGBONE BRICK PATTERN

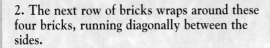

1. The key to laying a herringbone pattern is in the first four bricks. Starting in one corner, set the long side of the first brick across the corner at a 45-degree angle to the edging, and lean a second brick against it. Set a third brick at 90 degrees to the first, and a fourth brick between it and the edging of the second side.

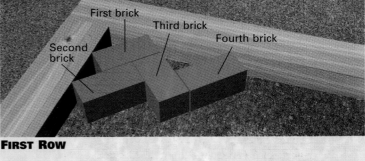

First brick
Third brick
Fourth brick
Second brick

FIRST ROW

2. The next row of bricks wraps around these four bricks, running diagonally between the sides.

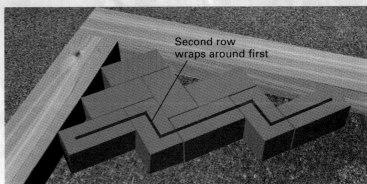

Second row wraps around first

SECOND ROW

3. Continue wrapping one row of bricks around the next, as shown. The rows will get progressively longer. Check periodically that each end of the row is equidistant from the corner.

Third Row
Fourth Row

PATTERN CONTINUED

4. When you've laid all the full bricks, cut partial bricks to fit in the opening around the border.

Cut bricks to fit in openings

COMPLETED PATTERN

POCKET GARDEN PATIO

For those who love to garden, a walk-out patio located just beyond the kitchen door can be a place to grow flowers, herbs, and small vegetables. Pockets, or openings in the paving, make convenient garden beds which you can fill with good, rich garden soil as you're building the patio.

This 540 square foot walk-out patio is not difficult to lay out, because it has an overall rectangular shape encompassing the similarly proportioned garden beds. The patio measures 18 feet by 30 feet and contains six garden beds, each measuring about 3 feet by 5 feet.

Constructing the patio with brick pavers makes it easy to incorporate the planting pockets into the overall plan. Each pocket is lined with the same 6×6 ground-rated pressure-treated timbers used to edge the rest of the patio.

When you plant your gardens, keep in mind that annuals and herbs will fare well in the pocket gardens, while deep-rooted vegetables and perennials are best grown elsewhere.

MATERIALS LIST

Element	Quantity*	Material	Length
Base			
	1.5 cu yd	top soil	
	9 cu yd	crushed rock or class 5 gravel	
	465 sq ft	weed-blocking fabric	
	3 cu yd	washed sand, concrete grade	
Edging	20	6×6s	10'
Brick pavers	2,250	4×8×2¼" bricks	

*All quantities may vary with site conditions.

TOP VIEW

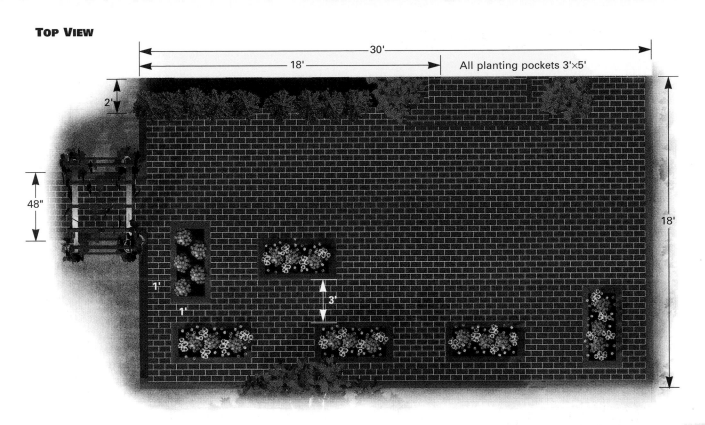

30'

18'

All planting pockets 3'×5'

2'

48"

18'

1'

1'

3'

BUILDING THE PATIO

Plants can't grow well in sand or gravel, so before you build the base, you'll stake and edge the garden pockets so they don't fill up with base material. Once that's done, you'll build the patio around the beds in the same manner as any sand-bed surface.

Begin by staking an 18-foot by 30-foot area for the patio. Excavate the patio area deep enough to handle a 4-inch to 6-inch gravel subbase if needed, a 2-inch thick sand setting bed, a layer of landscaping fabric, plus the thickness of 4 by 8-inch brick pavers. For more detail, see **Laying Out and Excavating the Site** on pages 18-19.

GARDEN POCKETS: Lay out the corners of each 3-foot by 5-foot planting pocket with stakes and mason's line. Edge the pockets with 6×6 pressure-treated timbers rated for ground contact. You can make the corners of the planting pockets by butting the ends of the timbers together but the corners will look better, and be stronger, if you cut half-lap joints like the one shown in the **Corner**

PLANTING POCKET

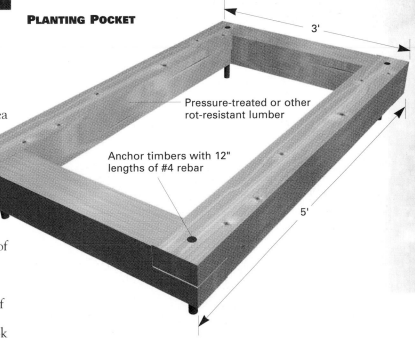

3'

Pressure-treated or other rot-resistant lumber

Anchor timbers with 12" lengths of #4 rebar

5'

POCKET GARDEN PATIO
continued

CORNER DETAIL

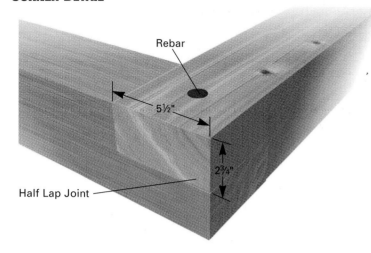

Rebar

5½"

2¾"

Half Lap Joint

Detail, above. Lay out the joints with a heavy pencil, and cut with a chain saw. Anchor the timber edging with 12-inch lengths of #4 rebar. Tamp at least 2 inches of garden topsoil into the planting pockets to keep the gravel from slipping under the timbers and finish by filling the planting pockets with potting soil.

PATIO BASE: Place 6×6 pressure-treated timber edging along the layout lines at the perimeter of the patio, but do not stake it yet.

Lay down and tamp the gravel base if one is needed. Cover the gravel with weed-blocking fabric and top it with a 2-inch-deep layer of sand. Strike the sand smooth. If the soil in your area drains well, and you don't need a gravel base, seat the edging in a 1½-inch-deep trench. A 2-inch layer of sand will put the bricks flush with the top of the edging.

Any brick pattern will work, although those at an angle to the perimeter will involve tremendous amounts of cutting and fitting. See the next page for ideas for paving patterns. Set the first course of bricks in a line parallel to the house and along an edge of the outermost planting pockets, leaving a ⅛ inch or less space between them. Work from that line toward the house. Complete the paving from that line outward toward the perimeter of the patio. Move the perimeter edging to fit snugly against the pavers and stake it in place.

When all the bricks are laid, and the edges are set, sweep fine sand between the joints. Wet and repeat the process until the joints are packed full. Fill the gap outside the perimeter edging with soil, and tamp it down. Top with sod or bedding plants.

PATIO CROSS SECTION

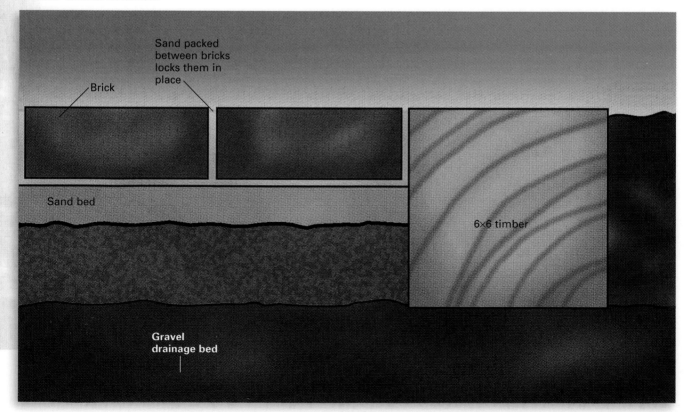

Sand packed between bricks locks them in place

Brick

Sand bed

6×6 timber

Gravel drainage bed

COMMON BRICK PATTERNS

One of the advantages of paving with brick is its versatility. Its rectangular shape allows it to be arranged in many different patterns. Some of the most common patterns are shown below, but they can be combined with each other, set at angles to the perimeter, combined with dividers of different materials, and arranged to produce a variety of patterns.

BRICK PATTERNS

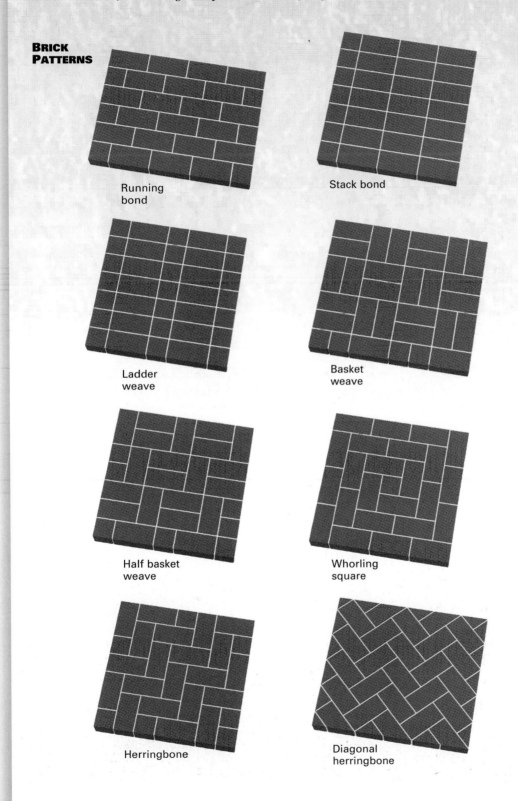

Running bond

Stack bond

Ladder weave

Basket weave

Half basket weave

Whorling square

Herringbone

Diagonal herringbone

GARDEN COURTYARD

Don't box yourself in when you're building a patio. Modern materials simplify making curves—including those in this circular patio inspired by the classic Celtic cross. The patio itself is set on a sand bed, eliminating the need for complicated curved concrete forms. And while the surface looks like cobblestone, it's actually made from pavers designed for jobs like this. Cast to look like stones, they're also shaped like a keystone, so you can lay the pavers in a circle without having to cut angles on the ends. When you come to one of the garden beds that give this patio its character, simple flexible plastic edging, shown on page 56, bends quickly to the desired radius, and holds the pavers in place.

Set in the center of a flower and herb garden, the patio consists of a nearly 30-foot-diameter core surrounded by circular planting rings. Four pathways, clearly marked by a change in the paver pattern, cut across the circle, leading to an inner circle with comfortable benches and a bird bath.

The benches and bird bath can be purchased ready made. While there are several well-made trellises that you could buy to place at the main entrance, the patio instructions include directions for the one shown here. It's designed with the moderately experienced do-it-yourselfer in mind.

**TOP
VIEW**

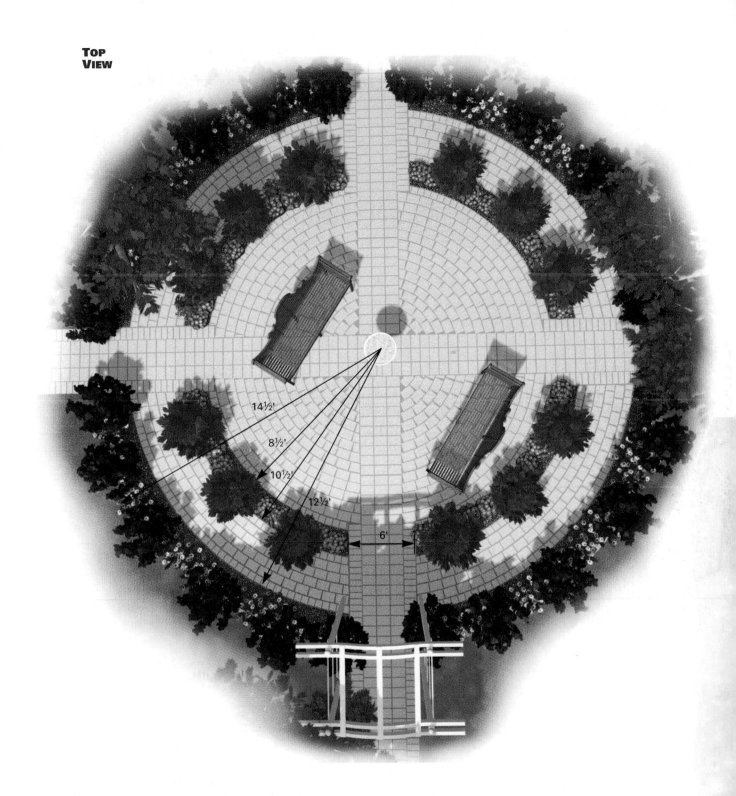

14½'

8½'

10½'

12½'

6'

BUILDING THE PATIO

Lay out a series of circles that mark the different parts of the patio. Begin by driving a stake in what will be the center of the patio. Tie one end of a rope to the stake. Tie the other end to a squeeze bottle filled with lime. Pull the rope taut and walk around the stake, squeezing the bottle to mark the ground as you go. Lay out the outside edge of the patio with the bottle tied 14½ feet from the stake; then draw circles with radii of 12½, 10½, and 8½ feet to lay out the rest of the patio. Lay out the ends of the beds by stretching two lines at right angles across the patio. Measure 3 feet on each side of the lines to mark the ends of the beds.

GARDEN COURTYARD
continued

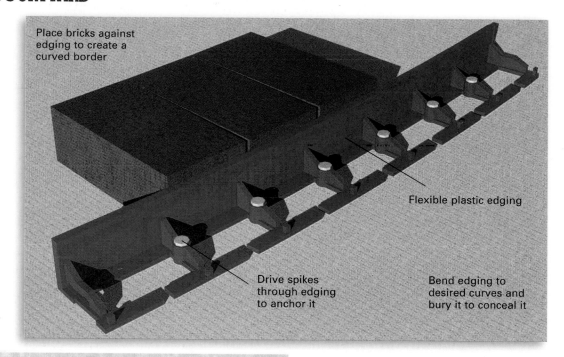

Place bricks against edging to create a curved border

Flexible plastic edging

Drive spikes through edging to anchor it

Bend edging to desired curves and bury it to conceal it

MATERIALS LIST

Element	Quantity*	Material	Length
Base			
	15 cu yd	crushed rock or class 5 gravel	
	4 cu yd	washed sand, concrete grade	
	2 cu yd	topsoil	
	227 sq ft	weed-blocking fabric	
Edging	343'	plastic patio edging	
Brick edging	1,200	4×8×2 bricks	
	Varies with style	Cobblestone pavers	
Purchased birdbath	1		
3'×6×8' TRELLIS			
Footings		gravel and concrete to build four 8"-dia footings to code	
Framing			
Posts	4	4×4s	12'
Arches	2	1×12s	12'
Side and top rails	6	1×3s	8'
Finials	4	Size as desired	
Fasteners		1½-inch deck screws	
		2-inch deck	

All quantities may vary with site conditions.

PATIO: Dig along the lime lines with a spade, excavating the patio and walkways. Before you set the pavers, you'll set the edging, made of bricks set on end (called soldiers), supported by buried structural plastic edging. Dig a bed deep enough to hold 4 inches of gravel, 2 inches of sand, plus the thickness of the pavers. Set the bricks against the edge of the excavation, push plastic edging tightly against them, and stake it to the ground.

Place gravel in the bed, tamp, and then cover with landscape fabric and 2 inches of sand. Set the cobblestone pavers over the sand in the pattern shown. When all the pavers are in place, sweep sand between them.

Remove sod from the area between the walks and fill with rich topsoil.

BUILDING THE TRELLIS

A trellis is probably the simplest garden structure to build. For this design, use 4×4 pressure-treated posts rated for ground contact. The sides are made of 1×4, the rafters of 1×2s, and the arched beams of 1×12s.

Place 4×4 posts in post holes so they are 8 feet tall, plumb, and squared with each other. The posts are 4 feet apart on center from one side of the arch to the other, and 3 feet apart side to side.

TRELLIS CONSTRUCTION

Top rail

Arched beams

Post

Side rail

8'

3'

4'

Make an arch pattern as shown. Cut four arches from a 1×12 board, following the pattern. Cut four more pieces from ¼-inch plywood, and screw the plywood to the solid stock for reinforcement.

Attach the arched beams flush with the tops of the posts. Then cut 1×3 rafters long enough to rest on top of the inner beams and meet flush with the outer beams. Set the rafters on edge and drill pilot holes through the rafters into the arches, and screw them in place with 1½-inch deck screws. Nail the side strips in place and attach a finial to the top of each post. Stain or paint the trellis, as desired.

ARCH TEMPLATE

Cut arch from 1×12

6'

2" squares

4"

16"

41"

TRELLIS DETAIL

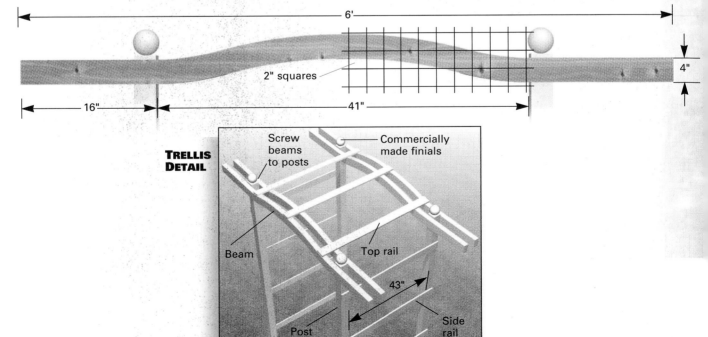

Screw beams to posts

Commercially made finials

Beam

Top rail

Post

43"

Side rail

HILLSIDE PATIO WITH RETAINING WALL

MATERIALS LIST

Element	Quantity*	Material	Length
18'×30' PATIO: FLAGSTONES IN MORTAR			
Base			
	10 cu yd	crushed rock or class 5 gravel	
	540 sq ft	reinforcing mesh 6-6-10-10	
Slab	7 cu yd (varies)	ready-mixed concrete, 4" thick	
Paving			
	540 sq ft	flagstone, cut irregular shapes, 2" thick	
	81 bags	mortar, type N mortar mix, 60-lb bags	
LANDSCAPE BLOCK RETAINING WALL			
	3 cu yd	crushed rock or class 5 gravel	
STEPPING-STONE PATH, EACH 3'-SQ SECTION			
Base			
	28	12" to 24" layout stakes	
	12'	mason's twine	
	0.25 cu yd	crushed rock or class 5 gravel 0.12[n-]	
	9 sq ft	reinforcing mesh 6-6-10-10	
Forms			
Temporary forms	4	2×4s	3'
	8	12" to 24" stakes for temporary forms	
Slab	0.15 cu yd (varies)	ready-mixed concrete	
Paving	9 sq ft	flagstone, cut irregular shapes	
Mortar	2	60-lb bags type N mortar mix	

All quantities may vary with site conditions.

Hillsides present problems when building patios. Since patios require a flat surface, building on a hillside often requires extensive grading. Unfortunately, the grading often changes the landscape drastically, creating a patio that seems to have been plopped randomly on the landscape.

Make no mistake—this patio also requires extensive grading. But the patio that results is carved into the side of hill, and the landscape surrounds and protects it. For stability, the patio is built on a concrete base, but it's covered with dressed flagstone for a natural look. The wall is well within the ability of the average homeowner. It's made of interlocking landscape blocks that you simply stack on top of each other—no mortar required. (Note that in most communities retaining walls over 3 feet high must be built by a contractor, so check with your building inspector before you begin.)

The combination of a mortar-free retaining wall with mortared patio requires an order of work a little different from what you expect. You'll have to pour the base of the patio first, and then set the wall in place on the soil next to it. Paving the surface with the flagstones comes last. If you're building a patio against an already existing retaining wall, install isolation joint material before pouring the concrete base.

TOP VIEW

Landscape block retaining wall

30'

18'

BUILDING THE PATIO

Excavate for the patio, the walk, and the wall at the same time, making a cut that is no more than 36-inches deep for the back of the wall.

Allow a 1½-foot to 2-foot clearance for the retaining wall in addition to the 18-foot by 30-foot patio. Give this patio a greater slope than normal—½ inch per foot—with the high point in the corner where the retaining walls meet. Orient the slope toward the open corner opposite the walled corner. This will allow water that drains behind the wall to be channeled by the concrete slab toward both the open ends. Excavate to a depth that will accommodate a gravel bed if used, a 4-inch concrete base, ½-inch mortar bed, and ½-inch to 1-inch-thick dressed flagstones.

In most cases you won't need a gravel bed. You'll be able to build both the patio and the wall on undisturbed subsoil. Use a gravel bed only if the soil is very dense, has a high clay content, or is in an area with poor drainage. Place and tamp the gravel layer, if used, right up to the dirt wall. For the forms, use 2×6s that you have ripped to a full 4 inches wide. (A 2×4 is actually only 3½ inches wide and will not give you a thick enough pad.) Stake the forms to sit tightly on the ground or

EXCAVATING FOR A RETAINING WALL

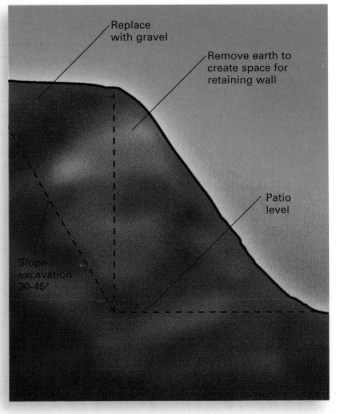

Replace with gravel

Remove earth to create space for retaining wall

Patio level

Slope excavation 30-45°

HILLSIDE PATIO WITH RETAINING WALL
continued

gravel base, so there will be no possibility of the concrete leaking out from under the forms and interfering with the retaining wall installation. Reinforce the slab with 6-6-6-6 mesh, and do not make control joints. Once the concrete is in place, scarify the surface—scratch it with a board into which you've driven nails about an inch apart. Mortar bonds more firmly with the rough surface this creates.

Make individual 3-foot by 3-foot concrete bases for the walk.

BUILDING THE WALL

Mortarless interlocking landscape blocks come in different sizes, styles, and functional designs—some have fiberglass pin connectors, others have overlapping flanges (see illustration, bottom). All of them, however, are designed to slope back into the hill to resist the natural pressure of the hillside.

Different manufacturers recommend setting the wall on different bases. Some recommend a well compacted gravel base; others prefer undisturbed soil. Follow the specific manufacturer specifications and instructions for the particular interlocking blocks you use.

In the area between the concrete slab and the dirt wall, lay landscape fabric over the gravel if used, or directly on the unexcavated subsoil. Place the faces of the blocks as snugly as possible against the edge of the concrete slab and level them side to side and front to back. After you've laid a few feet, check the

tops of the blocks with a 4-foot level. Put extra gravel under blocks that are too low and remove gravel from under ones that are too high. When the first row is done, shovel gravel into the void between the blocks and the dirt wall.

Set the second course of blocks on top of the first in a running bond pattern, with the upper block centered over the seam below. If you're using flanged blocks, put the lip of the flanged block over the back of the block below to give the wall its required slope. Align the holes in a pin-system block to create the proper slope. Shovel gravel behind the second course. Continue laying blocks and shoveling gravel. Fill in behind the last row of blocks with soil.

Cap the retaining wall either with solid units sold by the manufacturer to go with the specific blocks being used, or else with the same dressed fieldstone that is used to pave the patio surface. Attach the caps with concrete adhesive or mortar. Backfill behind the caps with topsoil, and then plant a ground cover.

Sweep mason's sand into the joint between the retaining wall and the concrete pad. Moisten and repeat until the joint is packed full.

PAVING THE PATIO

Finish by paving the patio with flagstones, set in a mortar bed. The patio shown has rectangular stones that were purchased

FLANGED-BLOCK WALL

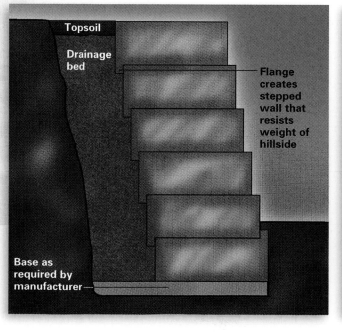

Topsoil

Drainage bed

Flange creates stepped wall that resists weight of hillside

Base as required by manufacturer

PINNED-BLOCK WALL

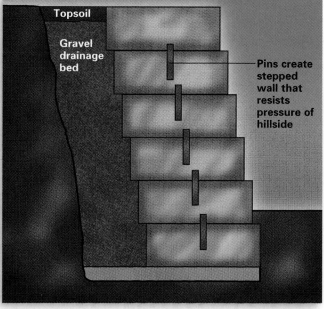

Topsoil

Gravel drainage bed

Pins create stepped wall that resists pressure of hillside

BACKFILLING BEHIND WALL

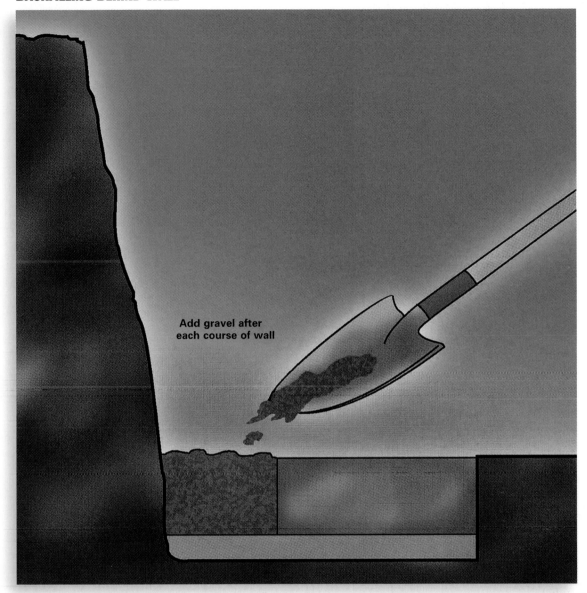

Add gravel after
each course of wall

pre-cut. The rectangular stone matches the shape of the landscape blocks. Stones with natural edges would also work, and would give the patio a less formal, more natural look.

No matter which type of stone you choose, begin by piecing the stones together on the patio, arranging them to fit together with joints no more than ½ inch wide. When you're happy with the way they fit, number the stones with chalk, so you can put them in order again later. Remove the stones and set them aside.

The mortar bed for a patio stone should be about an inch thick, flat, and uniform. Mason's usually set guides on the concrete base, shovel mortar between them, and then pull a screed across the guides to level the mortar. Set 1-inch O.D. pipes on the concrete for your guides, and shovel in enough mortar to cover a 3-foot-square area. Screed the bed flat, and begin laying stones. Depending on your skill and the drying rate of the mortar, you may find you can work with larger areas. Adjust the size of the area gradually, so that you don't have part of the mortar drying before you can get a stones on it. Butter the underside of the stones with thinned mortar, as described on pages 28-30.

Apply mortar between the joints, and wipe off any extra mortar with a burlap rag. After about a week, hose down the patio to wash off the haze left by the thin mortar residue.

PATIO WITH A FORMAL POND

A large, shallow pond gives architectural focus to this attractive patio. The pond is flanked on each side by a tiled patio measuring 15 feet by 18 feet. The total patio area is 540 square feet of paved space—684 square feet including the 8-foot by 18-foot pond.

This patio has dark ceramic tile borders and matching strips that visually divide each patio into four areas. The tiles also border the pond, emphasizing its shape and unifying the total setting. In areas with heavy winters, tile may be a poor choice of material—substitute milled flagstone.

Because tiles must be supported by a concrete base, you'll pour the base first, leaving an opening in the middle for the pond. Once the concrete is in place you'll make the pond by lining the opening with a flexible waterproof liner. After the pond is lined, you tile the patio.

Fountains in the pond add sparkle and life—and aerate the water—while perimeter plantings screen and shelter the patio and soften its contour. You will probably need the services of a professional electrician to install GFCI (ground fault circuit interrupter) outlets in the garden to run the fountain pumps. Pond maintenance varies by climate and seasons; consult a local pond supplier to determine whether plumbing or sewer utilities are required or desirable for a pond in your area. If needed, have the lines roughed-in by professionals during layout and excavation. Have them complete the work after the patio is built.

TOP VIEW

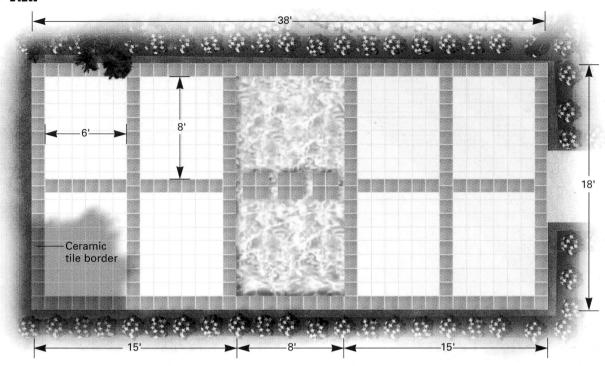

Ceramic tile border

BUILDING THE PATIO

Grade and stake the pond and the patio at the same time, following the basic instructions for **Laying Out and Excavating the Site** on pages 18-19. The surface of the patio should be no more than ½ inch above grade; excavation must be deep enough to accommodate a 4-inch compacted gravel bed, a 4-inch thick concrete slab, a ½-inch mortar bed, and the thickness of the tiles. Each patio must slope from the pond at the rate of 2 inches for every 8 feet of surface so that rain and garden runoff don't drain into the pond. If you're building the patio near a house, position the patio so water doesn't drain into the house.

EXCAVATING FOR THE PATIO

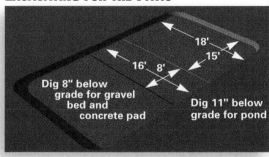

Dig 8" below grade for gravel bed and concrete pad

Dig 11" below grade for pond

After the general excavation, lay out the 8-foot by 16-foot pond with batter boards and string. Dig a space for the pond 3 inches deeper than the surrounding patio and 4 inches wider on each side than the finished pond dimension.

MATERIALS LIST

Element	Quantity*	Material	Length
Base			
	15 cu yd	crushed rock or class 5 gravel	
	540 sq ft	reinforcing mesh, 6-6-6-6	
Slab	7 cu yd thick (varies)	ready-mixed concrete, 4"	
Tiles			
	375	ceramic tiles, 12" sq	
	260	ceramic tile trim, 12" sq	
	8	60-lb bags type N mortar mix	
8'×16' POOL			
	1	Flexible pond liner, 14'×24'	
	2	Pond liner protection fabric, 8'×36'	
	12	Concrete blocks, 8"×16"×8"	
	1	60-lb bag type N mortar mix	
	12	Concrete pavers, 12"×12"	
	1	GFCI exterior outlet	
	2	Submersible pump with fountain	
	As needed	Concrete blocks to hold pump and fountain apparatus	

*All quantities may vary with site conditions.

PATIO WITH A FORMAL POND
continued

Set 2×12 forms into the pond excavation about 4 inches from the sides of the patio. The forms will keep the gravel out of the pond during the next step and create the edges of the pond when you pour the concrete. Stake and brace the boards on the inside of the pond, but don't nail them together.

Place and compact a 4-inch gravel bed, if one is needed, inside the patio excavation, but not inside the pond opening. Keep the gravel about 10 inches away from the pond forms. Stake and brace the forms around the patio perimeter. Caulk any gaps between the forms at the corners.

Follow the basic instructions for building a concrete base on pages 24-26. Reinforce the slab with 6-6-6-6 mesh, and reinforce the edge of the pond with ½-inch rebar. Do not make control joints in the surface of the slab.

BUILDING THE POND

After the concrete slab has hardened, remove the forms inside the pool and make the dirt bottom of the pool as smooth as possible. If necessary, fill depressions in the soil with dry sand tamped into place.

Install a strip of liner protection fabric on the bottom of the pond, positioned under the location of the stepping stones. Next, warm up the flexible pond liner in the sun to soften it. Get a group of helpers together and float the liner over the pond—like a parachute. After it starts to settle into the pond, loosely weight the edges of the liner with stones to keep the liner in place. Allow plenty of slack so the liner can settle all the way into the corners.

Normally, you would fill a pond with water to help push the liner into place in the corners, but this pond has to stay dry while you build the stepping stones. Instead of filling the pond with water, work in soft, clean shoes and carefully sweep the dry liner into place from the center of the pond toward the edges. Fit the liner up over the edges, pleating it in the corners. Weight the edges temporarily.

PATIO FORMS

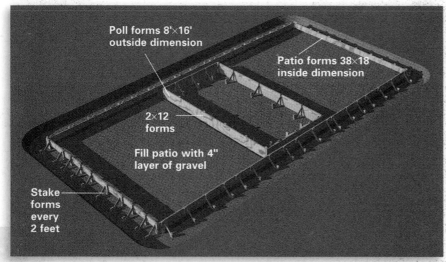

Poll forms 8'×16' outside dimension

Patio forms 38×18 inside dimension

2×12 forms

Fill patio with 4" layer of gravel

Stake forms every 2 feet

PATIO CONSTRUCTION

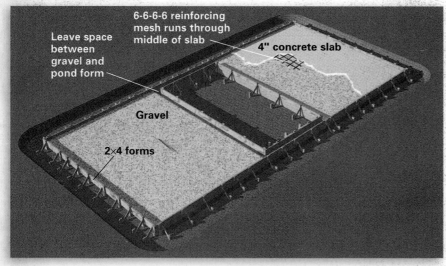

6-6-6-6 reinforcing mesh runs through middle of slab

4" concrete slab

Leave space between gravel and pond form

Gravel

2×4 forms

CROSS SECTION

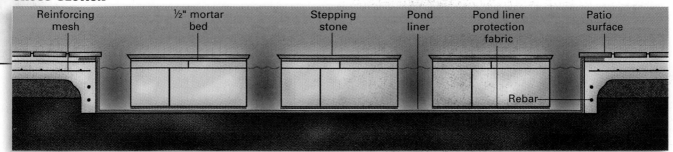

Reinforcing mesh | ½" mortar bed | Stepping stone | Pond liner | Pond liner protection fabric | Patio surface

Rebar

STEPPING STONES: Work carefully to prevent damage to the pond liner. Lay a strip of liner protection fabric 26 inches wide by 8 feet long across the center of the pond bottom. (To protect the liner while working, lay down a wider piece to walk on and trim it after the stones are completed.) Make a base for each stepping stone by mortaring four concrete blocks together, as shown. Fill the center with concrete and screed it to create a flat surface. Cover each base with four 12-inch square concrete patio pavers set in mortar. Work carefully to avoid getting mortar on the flexible pool liner.

Set bricks or concrete blocks, if required, on pieces of liner protection fabric on the bottom of the pond to hold submersible fountain pumps. Pumps are available at pond, pool, and aquarium suppliers.

After the stepping stone mortar is set, fill the pond with water to just below the surface of the stepping stones. The weight of the water will push the liner into place. Now smooth and trim the liner so it lays up and over the edge of the pool about 5 inches.

Starting ½ inch from the edge of the pond, spread a ½-inch layer of mortar for the 12-inch square accent tiles that go around the pool. Spread the mortar on top of the liner. Work in small sections at a time, setting the tiles so they are flush with each other and with the edge of the pool. Bed the tiles with a board and rubber mallet.

Working in small sections, tile the remaining surface of the patio in a ½-inch mortar bed, with the accent tiles arranged according to the plans. After a day, fill the joints between the tiles with mortar. Immediately clean off the tiles by wiping them with burlap.

STEPPING STONE BASE

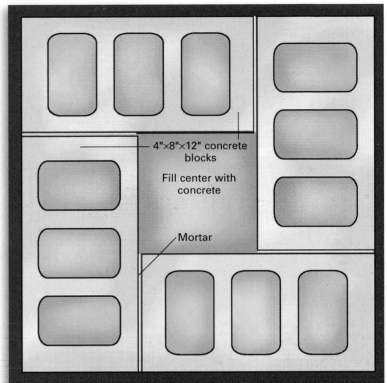

4"×8"×12" concrete blocks

Fill center with concrete

Mortar

STEPPING STONE CONSTRUCTION

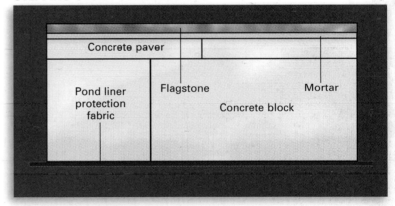

Concrete paver

Pond liner protection fabric

Flagstone

Mortar

Concrete block

PUMP INSTALLATION

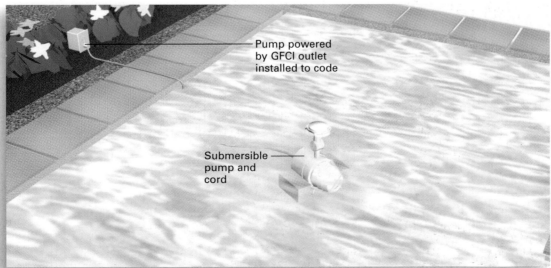

Pump powered by GFCI outlet installed to code

Submersible pump and cord

TWO-LEVEL PATIO

The levels of this patio break it into well-proportioned sections, creating a convenient eating area close to the house and an attractive sitting area adjacent to the yard and garden. The plan is well-suited to a yard that has a modest natural slope—a little regrading puts both sections of the patio at ground level.

If you so desire, you can tint concrete with a powder applied after the pour. However, it is much easier to order tinted concrete ready-made from your supplier. If you'd like a brick or cobblestone look—without the work—you can tint the concrete and stamp it with a grid available at masonry suppliers and home centers

The patio is tucked into the corner of an L-shaped house, like the patio in the Courtyard Patio and Arbor, so it has a high degree of natural privacy as well as an intimate relationship with the dwelling itself.

The number of steps from the house and between levels can be increased or omitted outright as a specific house and yard require. You'll build this patio as three distinct projects, starting with the upper slab, followed by the step, and finally the bottom slab.

MATERIALS LIST

Element	Quantity*	Material	Length
Base			
	10 cu yd	crushed rock or class 5 gravel	
	540 sq ft	reinforcing mesh 6-6-10-10	
Slab	7 cu yd (varies)	tinted ready-mixed concrete**	
	1	stamping pad for brick pattern	

*All quantities may vary with site conditions.

**As specified by concrete dealer.

TOP VIEW

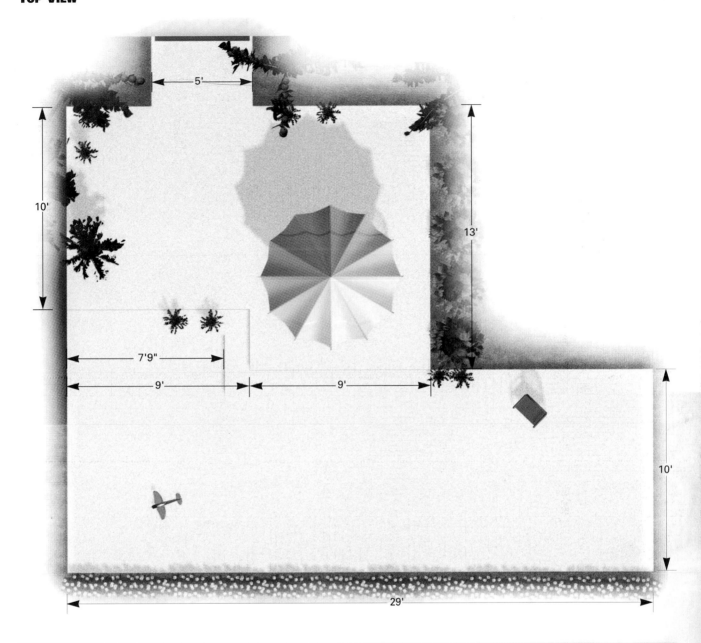

BUYING CONCRETE

Because this patio requires a large amount of concrete for a do-it-yourself project, you'll want to buy the concrete from a ready mix concrete supplier and have it delivered. If you want to mix the concrete yourself don't try to mix it by hand, rent a power mixer.

Concrete companies in your area can be found by looking under "Concrete" in the yellow pages of your local phone book. Before you call the concrete company, make sure you've already excavated the site (see pages 18-19), your forms are built (see pages 20-27), and everything you'll need is at hand. You don't want to have a concrete truck driver cooling his heels while you run around fixing forms and trying to find tools.

The concrete truck will need to park fairly close to the patio in order to pour the concrete. Make sure there is access for the truck. You may want to lay boards down on the lawn if you don't want the truck to leave depressions. Also, look up to make sure there are no electrical wires or cables that will prevent the truck from getting to the site. Your utility company can disconnect these lines for a short period if need be.

If you simply can't get the truck near the patio site, make sure to have wheelbarrows and help to ferry the concrete to the patio. Pouring large slabs of concrete is not a one person job. Make sure to line up help before the truck arrives.

TWO-LEVEL PATIO
continued

BUILDING THE PATIO

A two-tiered patio like this one requires a separate excavation and pour for each of the levels, as well as for the step. Pouring the steps and each level separately creates three independent structures. If one level shifts as the ground settles, it won't crack the rest of the patio.

The work begins at the top, and goes down. Begin by staking out the perimeter of the upper patio. The nature of the excavation will depend on the grade near the house. If there is a gentle slope, you may be able to simply carve the upper platform out of the slope. If the grade is relatively flat, however, you may find yourself having to add gravel to create the upper level.

If you are carving the upper platform out of the grade, dig first, and place the forms second. Dig enough to accommodate a 4 inch pad, and a 4-6 inch gravel base if needed. If you have to build up the base, set the forms first to hold the new material. Add gravel in 4-inch layers, compacting each layer thoroughly before adding more gravel. Resist the temptation to use the dirt you remove from the lower patio to build up the upper level. It isn't stable enough, and will cause the patio to crack.

The height of the edge nearest the step depends on the rise between the step and the upper patio. The actual rise will depend on your site. It's typically 8 inches, but for information on accommodating your site, see **Concrete Patio Stairs**, pages 32-33. Whatever the rise, the form should be that high, plus 4 inches—the thickness of the concrete.

Forms this high are best made with ¾-inch plywood and staked every 2 feet with 2×4s. Install the forms, and check carefully that they are plumb. Once you're satisfied, reinforce the forms with kickers, as shown on page 64, and check again for plumb. The kickers keep the weight of the gravel and concrete from forcing the forms out of alignment. Spend time and care building the forms. Improperly prepared forms can break after you've poured the concrete leaving you with a big mess to fix and much more work.

Once the forms are in place, excavate a trench about 4 inches wide along the inside of the form so the concrete will form a lip along the edge.

If the ground has a high moisture content or is subject to frost heave, put 6-6-6-6 mesh on top of the base, positioned so that it will fall in the middle of the concrete slab. (Get wire "chairs" designed for this purpose from your masonry supplier. Propping the mesh on brick or stones can seriously weaken the slab.)

Depending on your local construction codes, you may need to have the site inspected before the concrete is poured. If this is the case, be sure to have the inspection done a day or two before the concrete is to arrive in order to leave yourself enough time to modify the site according to the inspector's instructions. Call you local municipal building office to find out if an inspection is required.

Concrete is a great material for a split-level patio like this one. The texture and color unify the appearance, while the changes in level add interest.

This is also a patio, however, that lends itself well to the stamped brick technique. The concrete can be tinted red, and a brick pattern stamped into it after it's poured. The results create the look of brick without nearly

WHERE YOU LIVE MAKES A DIFFERENCE

If you live in a hot region or any area with intense sunlight, it is worth your while to investigate how you want to finish the surface of your concrete patio. An uneven, or mottled surface, such as some of those shown in **Special Concrete Finishes** on page 27, can substantially decrease how hot the concrete gets when it's exposed to direct sunlight. A cool patio on a hot day might substantially increase how much you enjoy the patio.

The temperature and region where you live also can have a large impact on how what type of concrete you buy and how you pour it.

If you live in an area that is subject to freezing temperatures in winter and hot temperatures in summer, ask your concrete supplier about air-entrained concrete. This special mix of concrete resists wildly fluctuating temperatures and using it may extend the life of your patio.

The temperature on the day you pour the concrete also may indicate the use of additives. If the day is particularly cold you pour, you may want to investigate the use of calcium chloride to cause the concrete to set faster. If the weather is hot you may want to have the supplier add a retarding agent so the concrete cures more slowly.

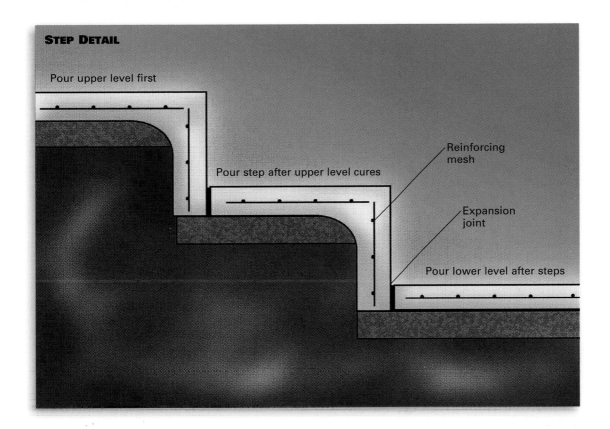

STEP DETAIL

Pour upper level first

Pour step after upper level cures

Reinforcing mesh

Expansion joint

Pour lower level after steps

the work. If you'd like to create the illusion of bricks, have the supplier tint the concrete red, instead of attempting to tint it yourself. Finish the concrete normally, and then stamp the surface with a grid that puts a brick pattern in the concrete. The grids are available at masonry suppliers and home centers.

Stamp a small area at a time. Put short sections of 2×6 on the concrete so that you can reach the areas you need to stamp. Wait until the concrete is sturdy enough to support you, but is still wet enough for the stamp to leave an impression. Begin stamping at a corner, and work from one edge to the other, always stamping over the area you were kneeling on.

If you've never finished concrete, the moment the truck shows up is not the time to learn. Either find a friend who has successfully finished concrete, or hire someone to finish the concrete for you. Also, make sure you've lined up enough help to ferry the concrete around in wheelbarrows while the finishing is underway.

Once you've poured and finished the concrete, cover it with burlap and keep the burlap wet for about a week, to prevent cracking as the concrete cures.

Building the step comes next. Put expansion joint material against the edge of the upper patio, as shown in the **Step Detail,** top. (A bead of construction adhesive will

hold it in place, if necessary.) The expansion joints keep the step and patio from bonding together, so that they can move independently if the soil shifts.

Make the form for the step from a piece of plywood, or use the plywood from the upper patio, if it's in good shape. Fill the forms with gravel to within 4 inches of the top forms, as shown in the **Step Detail**. (Again, depending on the terrain, you may be removing soil, or adding more gravel than shown.) Add the gravel in 4-inch layers, and tamp thoroughly. To give the riser some thickness, excavate a trench along the inside of the form that is about 4 inches wide and as deep as the form. Position reinforcing mesh, if necessary, and pour the concrete.

Now turn your attention to the lower patio. Place the gravel base, if any, and the forms. Place expansion joint material against the step riser—once again, because it will help prevent cracking. Place mesh, if necessary. Before you pour the patio, make sure you can get to it without disturbing the forms. If you'll be using wheelbarrows, build small ramps over the forms, using 1×6 and concrete blocks. Pour the first load of concrete up against the steps so that you won't be walking through wet concrete later in the operation. As always, dump one load of concrete against the next so that separate loads will mix seamlessly. Finish to match the step and upper patio, and allow the patio to cure.

WRAP-AROUND PATIO

This patio wraps around a corner of the house and steps down into a side yard to create a cloistered outdoor area adjacent to the house. It is sheltered by a fence with an open pattern that provides privacy without confining the space too much.

The arrangement shown creates a side patio readily accessible to the upper patio and house, especially the kitchen. This area is protected from public view and away from the livelier activity of the main patio. It could be a dining area or a private patio for a master bedroom, a home office, or the living quarters of a retired parent, depending on the access.

Wrapping a patio around the corner of a house makes it possible to take advantage of the light, sun, and breezes from several directions. The corner of the house also provides a way to separate the patio into distinct functional areas. The patio, as shown, is built on level ground. By varying the number of steps you could build the same patio into a sloped yard.

This patio is built of concrete pavers set in a sand bed. Pavers need an edging to hold them in place. In this case the edging is made of 6×6 beams arranged to minimize the amount of excavating you'll have to do.

BUILDING THE PATIO

It's unlikely that this patio will match your location perfectly. Begin by carefully planning the patio complex on graph paper to fit your yard. Include everything—the placement of the pavers, the size and location of the edging boards, and the width and placement of the fence panels—so that they fit together on your site exactly as you want them.

Follow the basic instructions for building a sand-set paver patio with permanent wood edging, (pages 20-23). Edge the upper patio with two layers of pressure treated 6×6 rated for ground contact. Level a bed for them on grade. Stake them in place with #4 rebar, driven 2 feet into the ground at the corners and every 4 feet in between. Edge the lower patio with a single layer of 6×6 set so the top is on grade. Lay gravel and sand beds that will put the pavers even with the top of the edging, and set the pavers in place.

TOP VIEW

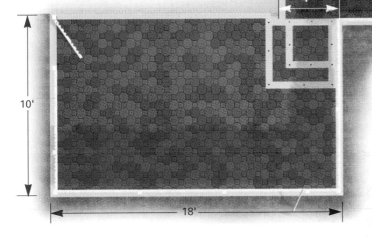

PATIO CROSS SECTION

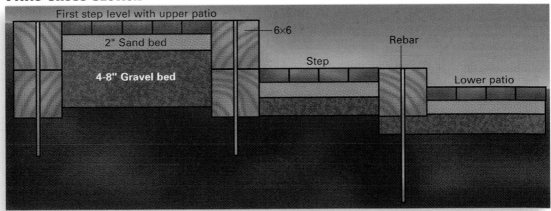

WRAP-AROUND PATIO
continued

MATERIALS LIST

Element	Quantity*	Material	Length
Base			
	7 cu yd	crushed rock or class 5 pea	
	540 sq ft	gravel weed-blocking fabric	
	4 cu yd	washed sand, concrete grade	
Edging			
Upper Patio	16	6×6s	10'
	8	6×6s	8'
Lower Patio	2	6×6s	12'
	2	6×6s	10'
	2	6×6s	8'
Stairs	4	6×6s	8'
	4	6×6s	10'
Rebar	28	#4	48"
	19	#4	30"
Paving	340	18"×18"×2" pavers	
PRIVACY FENCE			
Footings		gravel and concrete to build 8" to 12"-dia postholes to code	
Lumber, per panel**			
Post**	1	4×4	8'
Rails	2	2×4s	8'
Wide fence boards	3	1×6s	8'
Medium fence boards	4	1×3s	8'
Narrow fence boards	10	1×2s	8'
End posts	1	4×4	8'
Gate**			
Rails	1	2×4	8'
Brace	1	2×4	8'
Wide board	1	1×6	8'
Medium boards	1	1×3	8'
Narrow boards	1	1×2	8'
End boards	2	1×4s	8'
Fasteners	4 per panel	galvanized fence brackets	
	6d HDG nails	as needed	
	48 per panel	2" galvanized deck screws	
	1	gate latch	
	2	gate hinges	

All quantities may vary with site conditions.

**Use rot/insect-resistant lumber.*

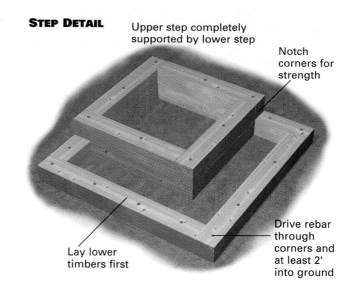

STEP DETAIL

Upper step completely supported by lower step

Notch corners for strength

Lay lower timbers first

Drive rebar through corners and at least 2' into ground

PATIO STEPS: The steps for this patio are boxes made of 6×6 ground rated, pressure-treated timbers. Make the box for the lower stairs—the exact dimensions depend on the paver you choose. Pick a size that keeps the number of pavers you cut to a minimum. Set a second, smaller box on top of the first. Support the floating edge with additional sections of timbers. Stake the timbers with ½-inch rebar long enough to reach at least 2 feet into the undisturbed ground. Fill the step centers with gravel, leaving room for a 2-inch sand setting bed, landscape fabric, and the pavers. Compact the gravel, line it with landscape fabric, add sand, and lay the pavers.

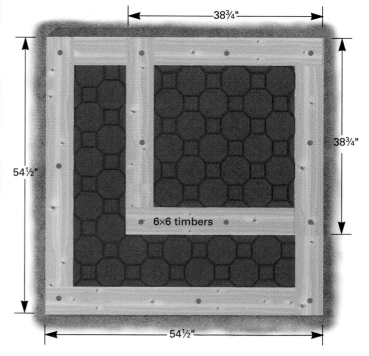

TOP VIEW, STAIRS

38¾"

38¾"

54½"

54½"

6×6 timbers

BUILDING THE FENCE

Lay out the fence with batter boards and line. Stake the positions of the posts along the line, setting them 6 feet on center, and dig holes for setting the posts. (The fence panels are designed to be 6 feet wide, but the panel dimensions can be adjusted to fit the available space. To prevent sagging, however, no panel should be longer than 6 feet.)

Set 4×4 fence posts rated for ground contact so they are 6 feet high. For more on fence posts, see **Posts, Piers and Footings,** page 31.

PANELS: Stretch a chalk line approximately 6 inches above the ground between the two end posts; level it with a line level, and snap the line to mark the posts. Set the bottom edges of galvanized fence brackets on these lines, and nail the brackets to the posts.

Lay out and install mounting brackets for the top rail, positioning them 12 inches below the top of the post. Working one section at a time, measure the exact distance between the two posts and cut rails to fit the brackets. Slip the rails into their brackets and nail in place.

Cut all of the vertical boards to their respective lengths. Screw the first slat to the rails, with 2-inch deck screws, plumbing it carefully. Cut a spacer to help you position the next slat. Continue attaching slats until the fence is complete, checking occasionally to make sure the slat is plumb.

GATE: To build the gate, screw the boards to the rails, as shown, with 2-inch deck screws. Add a diagonal brace cut to fit between the bottom rail and top rails. Attach the hinges to the gate, mount the gate on the gate post, and install the latch.

FENCE CONSTRUCTION

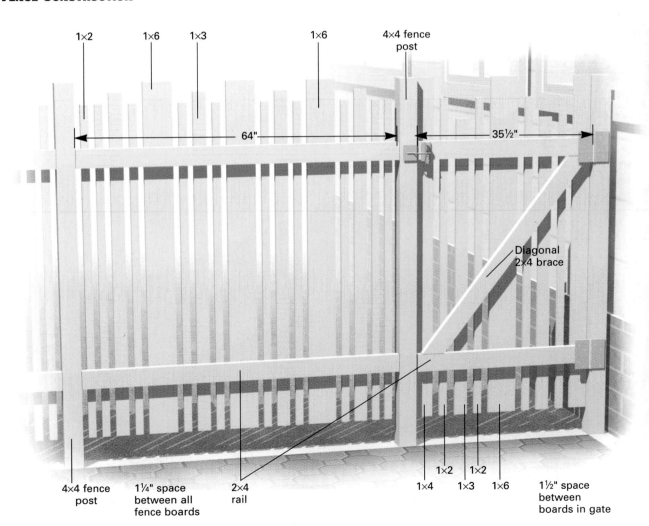

1×2   1×6   1×3   1×6   4×4 fence post

64"   35½"

Diagonal 2×4 brace

4×4 fence post   1¼" space between all fence boards   2×4 rail   1×2   1×2

1×4   1×3   1×6   1½" space between boards in gate

MULTI-LEVEL PATIO WITH SPA

A spa and a patio are a great combination, but making the spa look like part of the patio can be tricky. One solution is to set the spa above the surface of a flat patio. Unless there is a unifying structure, such as the overhead in the **Private Spa Patio** (pages 88-93), both the spa and the steps leading to it look like afterthoughts.

This split-level patio offers another solution. The spa is located on the lower level and placed against the upper level. Half the spa is reached from the upper level of the patio, so people can comfortably walk up to the spa, sit on its edge, and slip into the water. Putting the spa in this location provides easy access to the house for changing and getting towels. The mortar-set brick paving unites and emphasizes the solid construction of the entire complex.

TOP VIEW

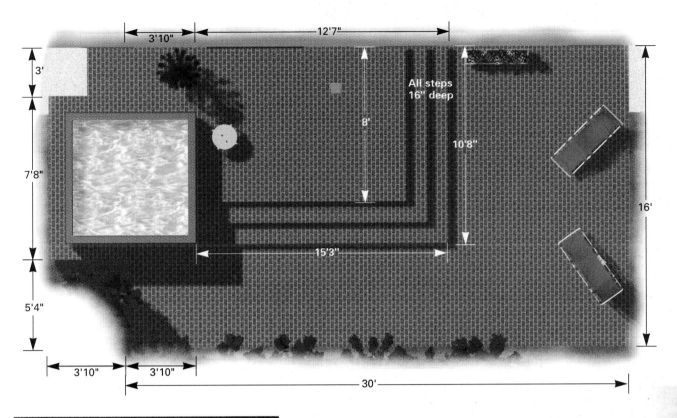

BUILDING THE PATIO

Pour this patio as two independent patios, following the basic instructions for building a concrete slab on pages 24-26.

Grade the top level first adding and tamping gravel to get the right elevation. Start by staking the corners and stringing guidelines. Dig deep enough, or add enough gravel for a 4-inch concrete slab, ½-inch mortar bed, and a layer of bricks at the right height. Then make an almost vertical cut around the top level no more than 16 inches deep. Make the cut inside the string lines a minimum of 4 inches to give the step between the layers some thickness. Cut a 90-degree notch out of one corner to make a bay for the spa. Next excavate for the bottom level, digging deep enough under the tub for a slab 5 inches thick—the minimum required to support the weight of a hot tub.

When the excavation is complete, but before installing the base, have a licensed electrician familiar with spa installation rough in a suitable underground circuit to the spa from the service entrance panel in your home. The outlet should be located in the mechanical area of the spa and equipped with a GFCI (ground fault circuit interrupter) outlet. The electrician will also wire grounding wires and bonding wires necessary to meet electrical codes. No plumbing hookup is needed because the spa is filled and drained with hoses.

Reinforce both the top and bottom slabs with 6-6-10-10 mesh. Rebar may be required near the edges of the top slab for additional strength; check your local codes. Build forms and pour the concrete in three stages, starting with the upper slab, followed by the steps, and finally by the slab.

MATERIALS LIST

Element	Quantity*	Material	Length
Base	10 cu yd	crushed rock or class 5 gravel	
	540 sq ft	reinforcing mesh 6-6-10-10	
	8 cu yd	ready-mixed concrete (varies)	
	34'	½"×4" expansion joint	
	23 sq ft	8 mil polyethylene vapor barrier	
Paving bricks	2,700	4"×8"×2¼" bricks	
	103	60-lb bags type N mortar mix	
		Purchased portable spa with cedar skirt, max. 7'8" sq, 36" deep	
		Underground 220-volt, 30-amp branch electrical circuit with GFCI	

*All quantities may vary with site conditions.

**For bracing sides of spa cutout.

MULTI-LEVEL PATIO WITH SPA
continued

CROSS SECTION FROM SIDE

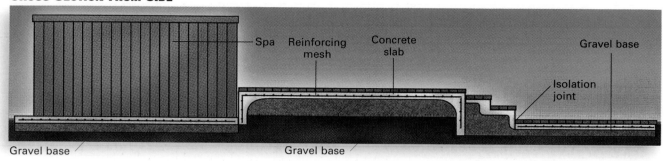

Spa   Reinforcing mesh   Concrete slab   Gravel base

Isolation joint

Gravel base   Gravel base

CROSS SECTION FROM END

Access panel   4" Concrete slab   Gravel base

Mortared brick patio

CROSS SECTION THROUGH STAIRS

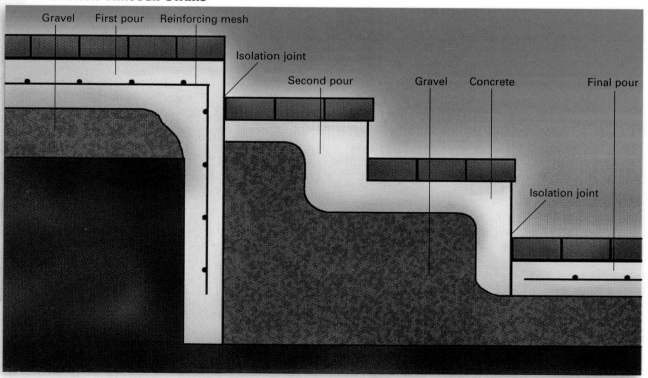

Gravel   First pour   Reinforcing mesh

Isolation joint

Second pour   Gravel   Concrete   Final pour

Isolation joint

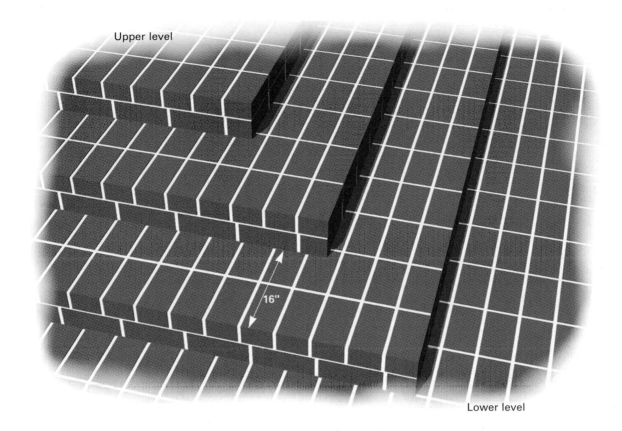

Upper level

16"

Lower level

UPPER LEVEL FORM: Place forms for the upper level. Most of the forms can be 2-by stock. The edge that steps to the lower level, however, will need to be 1-inch plywood that is well braced. Remove enough gravel to create a 4-inch-thick space between the gravel and forms. This creates a wall thick enough to support the upper level. When finishing, do not cut control joints in the concrete. Let the concrete cure in the forms for 3 to 5 days. Then carefully remove the forms and keep the concrete moist for several more days.

STEPS: The steps must sit on the same base as the patio, so build them before pouring the lower patio. You'll find basic step-making instructions on pages 32-33. In this case, however, keep the treads level and the risers plumb. Add the thickness of the finished lower patio to the height of the first riser. Stake the forms every 4 feet for support.

LOWER LEVEL FORM: Build the lower level a week after building the stairs. Install isolation joint material around the base of the upper level, the stairs, and along the house foundation. Cut a control joint in the concrete surface only between the spa area and the rest of the lower level.

PAVING: Pave the surface of the patio and steps with mortar-set bricks. (See page 28 for basic brick-laying instructions.) Do not pave over the control joint; bricks placed here are likely to crack. Lay bricks on either side of the control joint and fill the gap with flexible caulk instead of mortar. See **Common Brick Patterns** on page 53 for various brick patterns. The illustration above shows you how to apply brick over the steps.

INSTALLING THE SPA

Install flexible isolation joint material around the top edge of the concrete bay where the spa will be installed. Set the spa snugly against it with its access panel on an exposed side. Have a professional spa installer complete the installation and hookups according to the manufacturer's instructions and in accordance with local codes.

SPLIT LEVEL GARDEN PATIO

This split layout merges a house patio with a garden-filled yard. It draws the interior of the house into the outdoors via the attached 9-foot by 30-foot patio. A path connects this patio to a 12-foot by 23½-foot patio and a larger garden. There, an attractive garden seat-potting bench provides a place to sit and relax, or to do garden work with convenience.

Broad expanses of flagstone paving and free-flowing borders accentuate the close relationship between this patio and the garden setting. The natural stone, which is mortar-set on a concrete base, is a perfect complement to the natural environment of the yard. If desired, you can add a low picket fence to frame the garden area.

BUILDING THE PATIO

Excavate both patio areas and the walkway to the depth necessary to accommodate all the layers of patio materials: gravel, if used, a 4-inch concrete slab, ½-inch mortar bed, and ½- to 1-inch thick flagstones.

Then, stake the locations for the six potting bench posts in the garden-area patio. Build footings and piers with post anchors (see page 31 for techniques). After the piers have hardened, wrap expansion joint material around them.

Lay out and stake forms for the slab that supports the flagstone. The slab is reinforced with mesh, as explained on pages 24-26 and there is no need for control joints. Set forms for the mortar bed, lay and level the mortar, and set the stones, working a small section at a time.

TOP VIEW

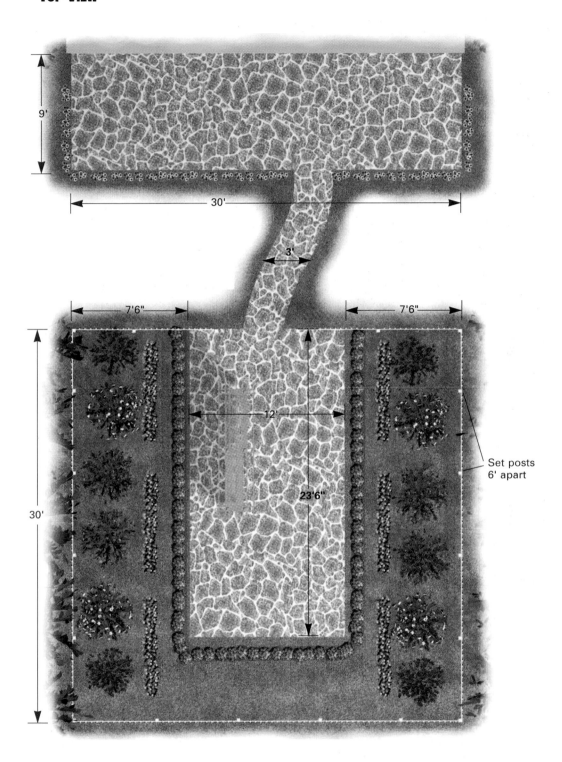

9'

30'

3'

7'6"

7'6"

12'

23'6"

30'

Set posts
6' apart

FENCE: Lay out the edges of the planting beds that surround the garden patio with batter boards and line. Sink 4 × 4 ground-rated pressure-treated fence posts around the beds, spaced as shown on the **Top View**, above. Nail 6-foot sections of prefab 3-foot-high cedar picket fence to the posts. Leave an opening for the walkway.

BUILDING THE POTTING BENCH/GARDEN SEAT

This potting bench/garden seat frame is built with ground-rated pressure-treated 4×4 posts, and pressure-treated 2×4s and 2×6s. The louvers are built of pressure-treated 1×4s. The seat slats are pressure-treated 2×2s. Standard shelving is used in the potting bench.

SPLIT LEVEL GARDEN PATIO
continued

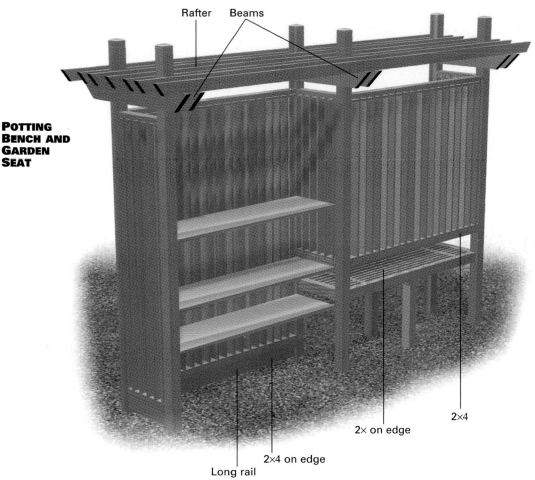

POTTING
BENCH AND
GARDEN
SEAT

Rafter   Beams

2×4

2× on edge

2×4 on edge

Long rail

FRAME: Pour the piers and footings before you pour the base for the rest of the patio. Wrap them with expansion joint material the next day and pour the base for the patio. You can begin work on the potting bench the next day. Chamfer the top of six 4×4 posts and cut them to 9½ feet. Install the posts in post anchors, using temporary braces to keep them upright and plumb. (See **How to Plumb a Post** on page 31.)

Cut six 2×6 beams 4 feet long, and angle the ends. Put a beam on each side of the posts—the bottom edges of the beams are level and 8 feet above the patio surface. Fasten them with ½-inch by 4-inch lag screws.

Cut eight 2×4 rafters 14 feet long.(If you're unable to get straight 16-foot 2×4s, you can make each rafter from two 8-foot 2×4s.) Cut an angle on the ends that overhang the unit. Set the rafters on the beams and fasten them with rafter ties, which are also sold as seismic or hurricane anchors.

LOUVERED PANELS: Make the louvered panels with the rails already in place. Cut

slats 5 feet long for the garden bench and center divider panels. Cut slats 7 feet long for the potting bench back and end panels. Position the slats with the help of 1×4 spacers 2¼ inches long. Begin by nailing a pacer to each rail so it is tight against the post. Set a 1×4 louver against the spacer, and nail through the rails to attach it. Continue nailing spacers and louvers to the rails until you've completed the panel. To keep the wide panels from sagging, support them with a long 2×4 installed on edge under the bottom rail, and attached to the posts with brackets. Screw the rails to the support approximately every 18 inches.

SEAT AND SHELVES

Make a 2×4 frame exactly wide enough and long enough to fit between the posts on the bench side of the unit. (The approximate measurements are 6 feet by 18 inches, but cut to fit the actual dimensions on your site.) Fasten 2×2s to 1×2 spacers with deck screws to make a seat, as shown, that fits inside the frame. Fasten the seat flush with the top of the frame by driving ½×3-inch lag screws through the frame and into the spacers.

SEAT DETAIL

1×2
Spacer
Seat fascia
Bench supports
Center support

LOUVER DETAIL

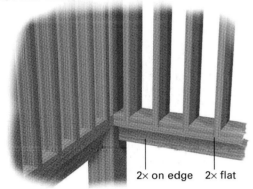

2× on edge   2× flat

Slip the seat between the posts so that it's flush with the outside of the posts. Build and attach the support as shown in **Support Construction,** below. Level the seat. Fasten it to the posts with ½×3-inch lag screws driven through the frame from under the seat.

Cut the shelves and worktable to fit and attach them with brackets to the front and back posts.

MATERIALS LIST

Element	Quantity*	Material	Length
Base	10 cu yd	crushed rock or class 5 gravel	
	10 cu yd	gravel	
	6 cu yd	concrete	
Paving	600 sq ft	Flagstone irregular shapes, 2" thick	
	90	60-lb bags dry-mortar mix	
	2	¼"×4"×8" expansion joint	
GARDEN SEAT AND POTTING BENCH			
Framing**			
Posts	6	4×4s	10'
Beams	6	2×6s	8'
Rafters	8	2×4s	14'
Long rails	4	2×4s	8'
Side rails	1	2×4	8'
Seat			
Fascia	2	2×4s	8'
Infill slats	10	2×2s	8'
Center supports	1	4×4	8'
Cleats	1	2×4	8'
Louvers	18	1×4s	8'
Spacers	1	1×4	8'
Bench rails	1	4×4	8'
Louvers	18	1×4s	8'
Bench spacers	1	1×4	8'
Bottom shelf	2	2×10s	8'
Worktable	2	2×10s	8'
Top shelf	1	2×12	8'
Fasteners	148	½"×4" galvanized lag screws, washers	
	2 lbs	8d HDG common nails	
	12	galvanized shelf brackets	
	6	post anchors	

All quantities may vary with site conditions.

**Use rot/insect-resistant lumber.*

SEAT CONSTRUCTION

1×2 spacers
2×2 bench slats
2" deck screws

SUPPORT CONSTRUCTION

Seat fascia
Center support
Cleats

WORKTABLE CONSTRUCTION

2×4 work surface
2×4 frame

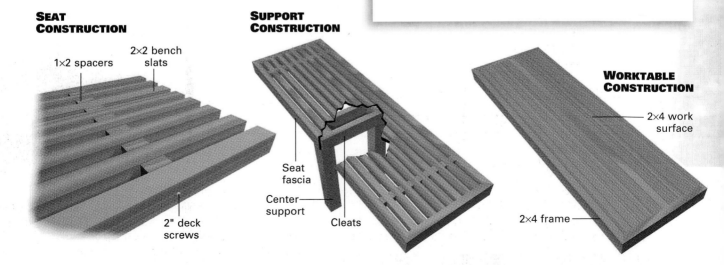

GARDEN COLONNADE

A long, sheltered walkway—or colonnade—provides an inviting transition between a patio next to a house and an inviting outdoor spot nearby—in this instance, a detached patio is a quiet corner of the garden. There, benches with built-in planters provide a comfortable place for visitors to sit and enjoy the scene.

The 4-foot-wide colonnade can be adjusted to any length and height needed between two seperate patios.

To visually tie the colonnade to the two sections of the patio, the large sand-set concrete pavers that make up the patio are laid in a random pattern throughout the colonnade. Plantings around the pavers turn the walkway into a garden as well.

TOP VIEW

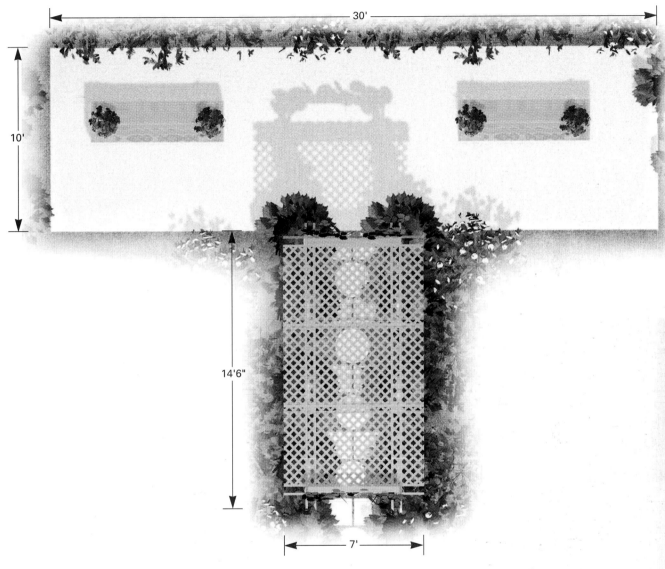

BUILDING THE PATIO

Follow the basic instructions for layout and excavation on pages 18-19 and paving a sand-bed patio on pages 20-23, breaking the patio into sections. The patio can be any size that fits the profile of your home and the terrain in your yard. The one shown in the plan is 9 feet by 18 feet, with a $14\frac{1}{2}$ foot stepping-stone walkway. Pave both the patio and walk surfaces with large concrete pavers—12 inches, 18 inches, or 24 inches square—with an incised or a textured surface.

Pavers are not meant to be used with mortar. See **Working with Pavers** on page 20 for tips on how to work with them.

GARDEN COLONNADE
continued

BENCH CONSTRUCTION

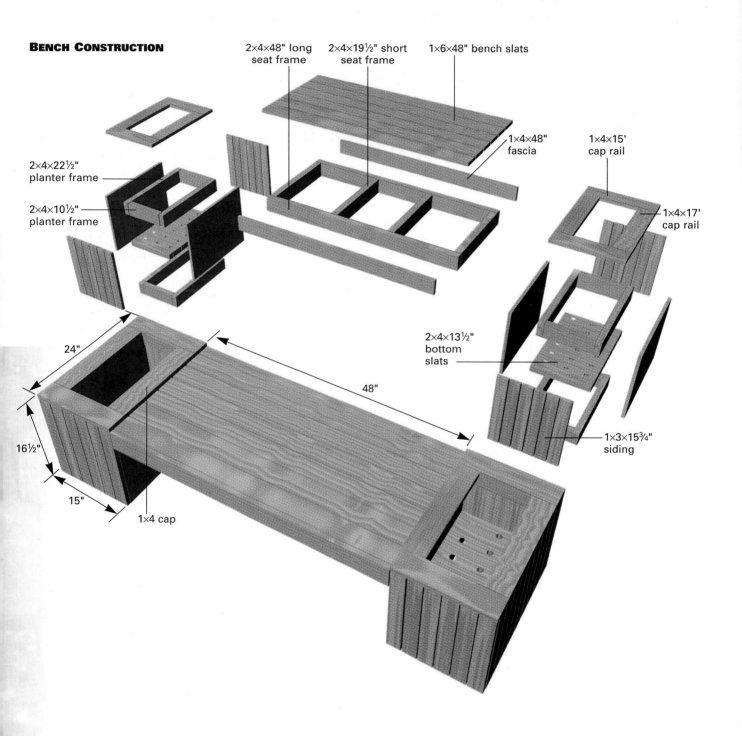

2×4×48" long seat frame

2×4×19½" short seat frame

1×6×48" bench slats

1×4×48" fascia

1×4×15' cap rail

2×4×22½" planter frame

2×4×10½" planter frame

1×4×17' cap rail

2×4×13½" bottom slats

24"

48"

16½"

15"

1×4 cap

1×3×15¾" siding

BUILDING THE BENCH

Build the benches for the detached patio area with heart redwood, cedar, cypress, or pressure-treated lumber. Construct the planters first; then build a bench seat and attach it to them.

PLANTERS: Screw together four 2×4 box assemblies, each 22½ inches long and 13½ inches wide. These are the top and bottom frames of the two planters.

Cut and nail 2×4s to the top of the bottom box assemblies to make floors on the two bottom frames. Leave gaps between the 2×4s and drill ½-inch drainage holes in a scattered pattern across the floors.

Cut the siding into 15¾-inch pieces. Screw one end of a piece to the corner of a bottom frame, and the other end to the corner of a top frame. Repeat at each corner, and then fill in between the pieces with siding. If necessary, rip pieces to fit.

SEATING PLATFORM: Make another 2×4 box assembly, this one 48 inches long by 22½ inches wide. Cut two 2×4s cross pieces to fit inside, as shown, and fasten them with 10d hot-dipped galvanized nails. Cut the fascia to length and nail them to the long sides of the box. Countersink the nail heads.

Cut six 1×4 slats to length. Space them as needed to fill the opening for the seat and nail them to the top of the frame with 6d hot-dipped galvanized nails.

Turn the planters upside down on a flat, level surface and center the seating platform between them. Drill two ½-inch diameter pilot holes into the seating platform frame through each of the box frames. Fasten them together with ½×6 inch hex-head bolts.

Turn the assembly right side up.

Line the insides of the planter boxes from the tops down with plastic sheeting, poking holes through it into the drain holes you made earlier. Staple the edges of the sheeting to the tops of the siding, and trim the excess. Miter a 1×4 cap molding for each box opening and nail it over the plastic.

MATERIALS LIST

Element	Quantity*	Material	Length
Base			
	7 cu yard	gravel	
	4 cu yd	washed sand, concrete grade	
	156'	plastic edging	
	540 sq ft	weed-blocking fabric	
Paving (size optional)			
	540	12"×12" concrete pavers	
	240	18"×18" concrete pavers	
	135	4"×24" concrete pavers	
Colonnade Framing			
Footings**		gravel and concrete to build 8 footings to code	
Posts	4	4×4s	12'
	4	4×4s	10'
Headers	8	2×6s	8'
Beams	4	2×6s	16'
Knee Braces	6	2×6s	8'
Rafters	8	2×4s	8'
Lattice panels	3		4'×8'
Bench (quantities for 1 bench)			
Planter frames	4	2×4s	8'
Planter bottom	2	2×4s	8'
Planter siding	10	1×3s	8'
Plastic sheeting***	as needed		
Planter trim	2	1×4s	8'
Seat			
Seat frames	2	2×4s	8'
Bench slats	4	1×4s	8'
Fascia	1	1×4	8'
Fasteners			
	1 lb	6d hot-dipped galvanized nails	
	1 lb	10d hot-dipped galvanized nails	
	4	½"×6" galvanized hex head bolts, washers	
	4	½"×4½" galvanized carriage bolts, washers	
	64	⅜"×4" galvanized carriage bolts, washers	
	8	galvanized post anchors	
	1 box	1" galvanized deck screws	

*All quantities may vary with site conditions.

**Use rot/insect-resistant lumber.

***To line sides of boxes.

GARDEN COLONNADE
continued

COLONNADE

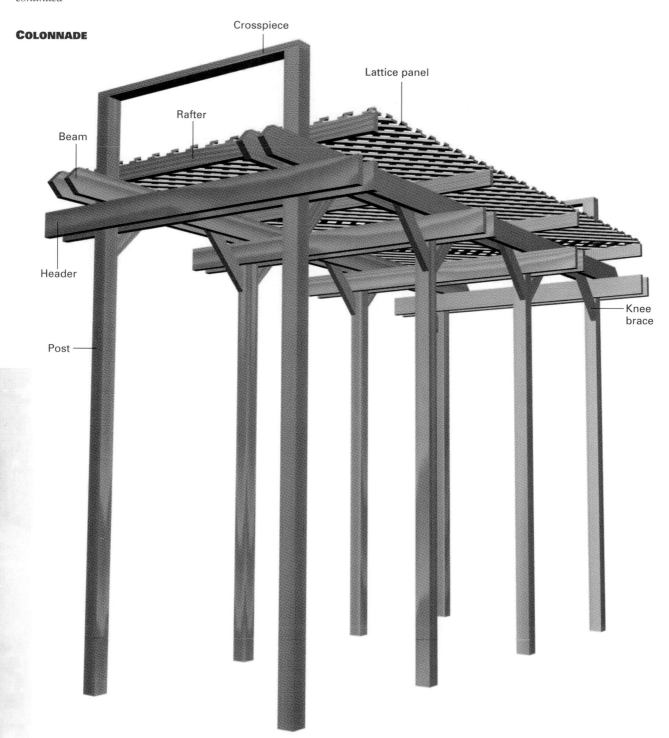

Crosspiece

Lattice panel

Rafter

Beam

Header

Post

Knee brace

BUILDING THE COLONNADE

Use heart redwood, cedar, cypress, or pressure-treated lumber to build this covered walkway between the patios. Pour eight footings-and-piers to support the posts as shown in the **Colonade Top View**. Make sure the piers are level, all the same height, and the post anchors are aligned with each other. Refer to page 31 for instructions on building post footings.

Place large concrete-block pavers in a random or formal pattern to form a stepping stone path through the colonnade.

COLONNADE TOP VIEW

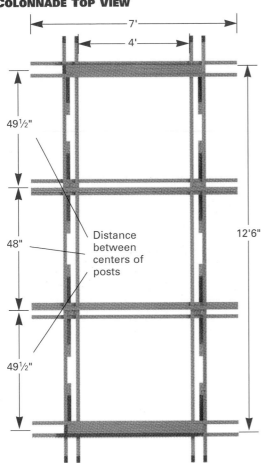

Distance between centers of posts

Because each paver is isolated from its neighbor, there is no need for a sand and gravel bed. Lay the pavers directly on the ground.

Cut four end posts 10½-feet long. Cut four interior posts 9-feet long. Install the posts in post anchors, using temporary braces to keep them upright and plumb.

Cut the headers, beams, and rafters to length. Drill holes in each for the ½×4-inch lag screws that will fasten them to the posts. Bolt 2×6 headers to both sides of the posts, 5½ inches below the tops of the interior posts and 23½ inches below the tops of the longer posts. Bolt 2×6 beams across the headers so they are flush with the tops of the interior posts and 18 inches below the tops of the end posts. Bolt a beam to each side of the posts and attach 2×6 knee braces that run between the posts and beams at a 45-degree angle with ⅜-inch lag screws. The temporary post bracing can now safely be removed from the sides. Drill pilot holes and nail 2×4 cross pieces to the top of the beams with 10d nails. Space the rafters 48 inches apart on center to support the edges of the lattice panels. If needed, trim lattice to fit, then screw the lattice panels to the rafters with 1 inch deck screws.

COLONNADE SIDE VIEW

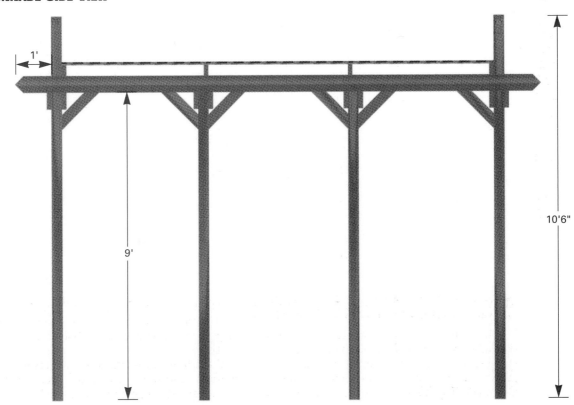

SPLIT PATIO WITH PRIVATE SPA

The main patio in this plan is 18×30 feet—the 540 square feet typical of the plans in this book. The spa patio adds another 170 square feet. Installing the spa on a separate patio preserves the larger patio space for more general family activities. The spa overhead, made with heart redwood, cedar, or pressure-treated lumber, has a cedar-sided privacy screen along the back. A prefabricated stairway is put in place after the spa is installed.

The two-patio arrangement has an economic advantage, too: the 5-inch-thick concrete slab required to support the weight

TOP VIEW

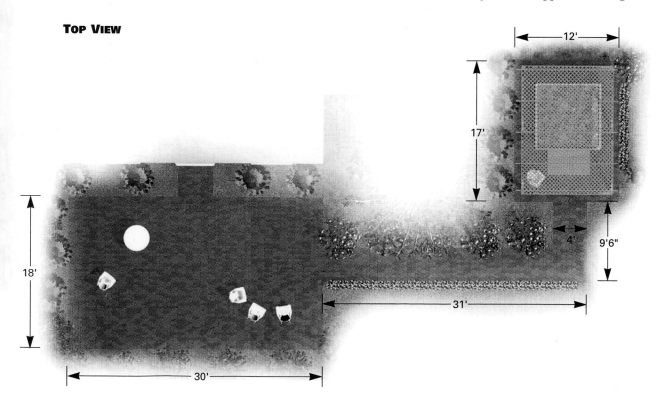

of the filled spa is necessary only in the spa section of the patio. In fact, the main patio and its path can be built with sand-bed paving as shown here.

Because the spa patio and main patio are built with different construction techniques, this is a good project to split into smaller mini-projects. You might do that for budgetary reasons or to make time for doing most of the work yourself in the evenings and on weekends. You can build the spa patio first and the main patio any time later. Or, if you have the electrical lines for the spa roughed in first, you can build the main patio one season and the spa patio the next.

BUILDING THE MAIN PATIO

Excavate and lay a sand-set main patio. Extend the excavation to include the pathway to the spa patio. If an electrical line from the main panel of the house needs to run under the main patio or walkway, have a licensed electrician rough it in now. For more information on building a sand-set patio see pages 20-23.

BUILDING THE SPA PATIO

Lay out a 12-foot by 17-foot patio for the spa. Excavate for the overhead post footings and for a 5-inch slab at the same time.

SPA OVERHEAD CONSTRUCTION

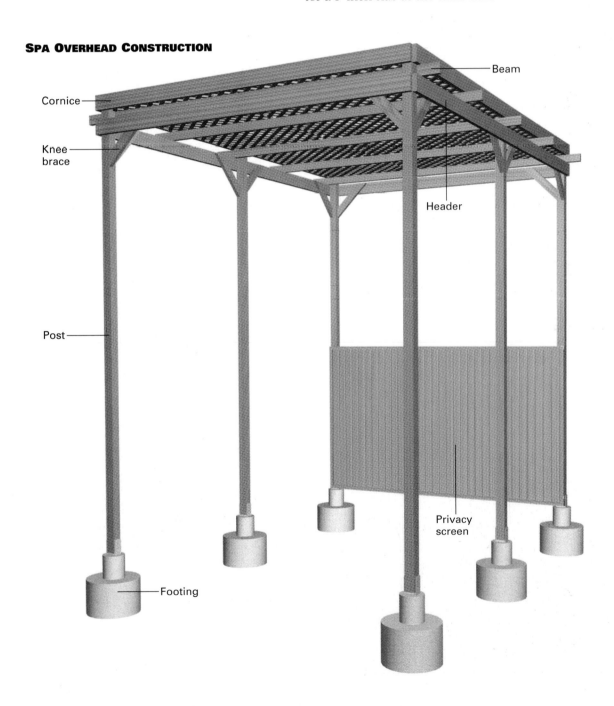

Cornice

Knee brace

Post

Footing

Beam

Header

Privacy screen

SPLIT PATIO WITH PRIVATE SPA
continued

TOP VIEW

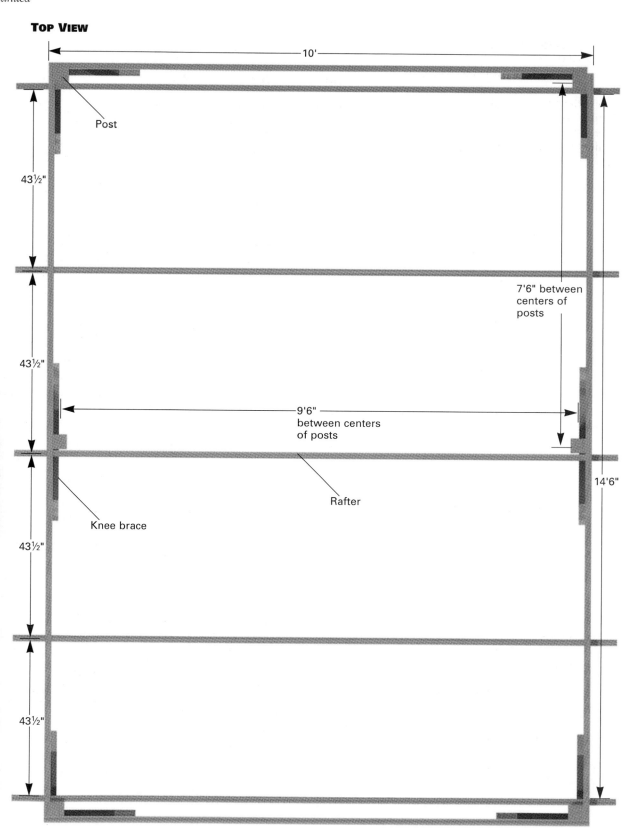

Post

43½"

43½"

7'6" between
centers of
posts

9'6"
between centers
of posts

Rafter

Knee brace

43½"

10'

14'6"

43½"

Stake locations for six post footings, three on either side of the patio.

When the excavation for the small patio is complete, but before installing the base, have a licensed electrician familiar with spa installation rough-in an underground circuit from the service panel of the house to the mechanical area of the spa. No plumbing hookup is required, because the spa will be filled and drained with hoses.

Pour the footings and piers and install post anchors, as explained in **Posts, Piers and Footings** on page 31. Make sure that the tops of the forms for the piers are all level, and that they are all the same height. To do this, lay a 10- or 12-foot straightedge on two pier forms and adjust the forms until the straightedge is level. Check the rest of the piers, always working from a leveled pier to an unleveled pier. After the footings and piers are poured, while the concrete is still wet, stretch mason's line across the piers. Use it to align the post anchors perfectly with each other.

After the footings are poured, prepare for the concrete slab. Rip 2×6s to make forms 5 inches high. Pour the slab and finish it with a broomed or slightly textured finish for slip-resistance with wet feet. Cut a control joint around the area that will hold the tub.

BUILDING THE OVERHEAD

Cut the posts 9½ feet long. Install the posts in post anchors set in the piers, using temporary braces to keep them upright and plumb.

Cut 2×6s for headers. Align the tops of the headers 9 inches below the tops of the posts. Attach them to the posts with ½-inch by 4-inch lag screws.

Cut the 2×4 beams to extend 10 inches beyond the headers. Space the beams evenly across the headers as shown in the **Top View**. Attach the beams with rafter ties, also sold as seismic or hurricane anchors.

Cut 2×6s to make a cornice around the top of the structure. Position them across the beams, flush with the tops of the posts. Attach them to the posts with ½-inch by 4-inch lag screws.

MATERIALS LIST

Element	Quantity*	Material	Length
18'×30' MAIN PATIO			
	10 cu yd	crushed rock or class 5 gravel	
	540 sq ft	weed-blocking fabric	
	6 cu yd	washed sand, concrete grade	
	76'	plastic edging	
	400**	18" sq pavers	
10'×17' SPA PATIO			
Patio			
	3 cu yd	crushed rock or class 5 gravel	
	170 sq ft	reinforcing mesh 6-6-10-10	
	3 cu yd (varies)	ready-mixed concrete	
Paving (optional)	125	18" sq concrete pavers	
	29	60-lb bags type N mortar mix	
OVERHEAD			
Framing*			
Footings and concrete to build 6 footings to code			
Posts	6	4×4s	16'
Short headers	2	2×6s	12'
Long headers	4	2×6s	14'6
Rafters	5	2×4s	12'7"
Short cornice	2	2×6s	10'7"
Long cornice	4	2×6s	14'6"
Lattice	6	4×8' panels	
Privacy-screen	22	1×6 siding	10'
Screen frame	8	1×2s	10'
Fasteners			
	6	galvanized post anchors	
	54	⅜ ×3" galvanized lag screws, washers	
	1 lb	8d hot-dipped galvanized nails	
Underground 220-volt, 30-amp branch circuit with GFCI			
Purchased 7'8"-sq spa with cedar skirting, insulated cover, and steps			

*All quantities may vary with site conditions.

**With a 4'×31' path.

***Use rot/insect-resistant lumber.

SPLIT PATIO WITH PRIVATE SPA
continued

CONSTRUCTION DETAIL

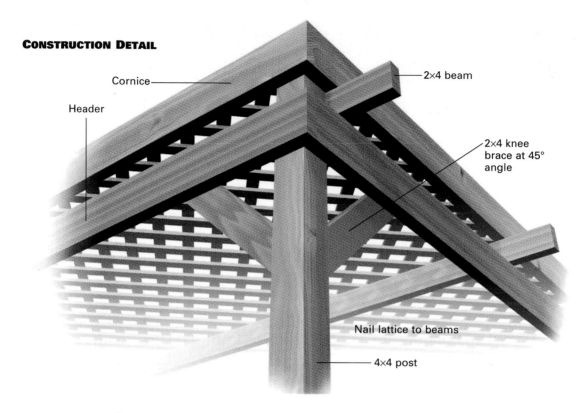

Cornice

Header

2×4 beam

2×4 knee brace at 45° angle

Nail lattice to beams

4×4 post

PRIVACY SCREEN DETAIL

Nail tongue-and-groove siding to 2×4 to make privacy screen

To stabilize the framework, attach 2×4 knee braces between the posts and headers at a 45-degree angle to the posts. Fasten the braces with ⅜×4-inch lag screws.

Complete the assembly by attaching lattice panels to the rafters at the top of the structure and installing the privacy screen.

BUILDING THE CEDAR PRIVACY SCREEN

Cut two ground-rated, pressure-treated 2×4s to reach from the outside edge of one back post to the outside edge of the other back post. Toe nail the 2×4s to the posts wide side up using 8d hot-dipped galvanized nails. Nail tongue-and-groove cedar siding to the back side of the 2×4s to create the panel. If desired, you can put 1×3s around the back edges of the panel to give it a more finished look.

FRONT VIEW

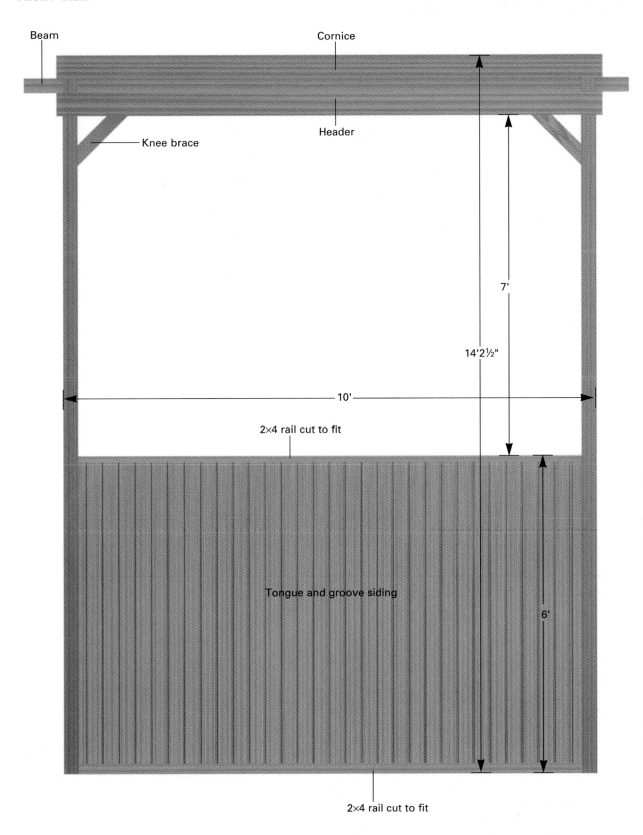

Beam

Cornice

Header

Knee brace

7'

14'2½"

10'

2×4 rail cut to fit

Tongue and groove siding

6'

2×4 rail cut to fit

GLOSSARY

Aggregate. Sand, crushed stone, gravel, or other material added to cement and water to make concrete or mortar.

Air-entrained. Concrete suffused with tiny air bubbles, making it more workable and better able to withstand frost. Air entrainment requires the addition of a special mixture during the mixing stage.

Backfilling. Replacing earth excavated during the construction process. A material other than the original earth may be used to improve the drainage or structure of the soil.

Bedding sand. Coarse sand, like that added to concrete mixes, used to make the bed for setting pavers or bricks.

Broom finish. A slip-resistant texture created by running a stiff broom across fresh concrete.

Bull float. A large, long-handled float used for reaching into the center and smoothing a large slab of wet concrete.

Butter. Applying mortar to stones or bricks.

Concrete. A mixture of portland cement, fine aggregate (sand), course aggregate (gravel or crushed stone), and water. Concrete becomes harder and stronger with age.

Concrete pavers. Preformed concrete units commonly used for driveways, patios, and sidewalks. Pavers are designed to be laid in a sand base. They come in many shapes and colors and may interlock in repeating patterns.

Control joints. Grooves that are tooled or cut into the surface of wet concrete to make it crack in straight lines at planned locations, rather than cracking randomly.

Curing. The process of aging a new concrete slab with proper moisture to reduce cracking and shrinkage and to develop strength.

Darby. A tool with a long sole made of smooth wood or metal, used for smoothing the surface of a concrete slab after initial leveling.

Edging. The rounded edges of a concrete slab that are resistant to cracking.

Excavation. Digging out earth to a level that is hard and uniformly graded.

Expansion joint. *See* Isolation joint.

Exposed aggregate. A decorative treatment that exposes a layer of stones embedded in the surface of concrete.

Finish. A coating applied to a surface to protect it against weathering, or a treatment such as texturing applied to concrete.

Floating. Smoothing the surface of soft concrete after it has been leveled. This action fills in divots and low spots and drives large aggregate below the surface. Floats may be made of steel, aluminum, magnesium, or wood.

Footing. The bottom portion of any foundation or pier. The footing distributes weight of the structure into the ground. For decks, it often refers to the concrete structure consisting of the pier as well as its footing.

Formwork. The wooden forms that shape wet concrete.

Frost heave. Movement or upheaval of the ground when there is alternate freezing and thawing of water in the soil. This is one of the reasons concrete slabs crack, making control joints necessary.

Frost line. The lowest depth at which the ground will freeze. It determines the code-required depth for footings.

Isolation joint. Strips of material installed in formwork to completely separate new concrete from existing construction or from other new construction. Allows sections to move independently of one another if the ground shifts because of factors like frost heave. Sometimes called expansion joints.

Jointing sand. Fine sand that is spread over brick pavers and swept into the spaces between them. It is often sold as Mason's sand.

Lag screw or bolt. Heavy-duty screw with a bolt head for attaching structural members to a wall or to material too thick for a machine bolt to go through.

Mason's line. Twine used to lay out posts, patios, footings, and structures. Preferred because it will not stretch and sag, as regular string does.

Mortar. A mixture of cement, fine aggregate, and water used to bond bricks, blocks, or stones.

Pavers. Preformed concrete or brick units commonly used for driveways, patios, and sidewalks. Designed to be laid in a sand base, they come in many shapes and colors and may interlock in repeating patterns.

Pier. A small concrete or masonry structure that holds a post off the ground. It has its own footing and can be precast or cast in place.

Plastic concrete. Concrete that has not hardened.

Portland cement. A type (not a brand name) of cement that is a basic ingredient of concrete and mortar.

Pressure treatment. A process of forcing preservatives into wood. One commonly used pressure treatment is waterborne chromated copper arsenate (CCA). CCA specified for above ground use is labeled LP-2 or .25 (pronounced "point two-five." CCA rated for ground contact is labeled LP-22 or .40 ("point four-oh").

Ready-mix concrete. Wet concrete that is ready to pour, transported in a truck from a concrete supplier.

Rebar (reinforcing bar). Steel rods for reinforcing concrete.

Reinforcing mesh. Steel wires welded into a grid of 6- or 10-inch squares and embedded in concrete. Ties a concrete pad together in the event of cracking.

Screeding. Dragging a straight 2×4 across wet concrete to strike off excess concrete.

Segregation. Separation of the elements of concrete, such as water rising to the top or aggregate sinking to the bottom due to overworking or bouncing (as in the motion of a wheelbarrow).

Soldier bricks. Bricks standing on end with the narrow faces exposed.

Troweling. Giving the concrete a smooth final finish with a steel trowel. This step is for interior applications, as it creates an extremely smooth and possibly slippery surface.

INDEX

Boldface numbers indicate pages with photographs or illustrations related to the topic.

METRIC CONVERSIONS

U.S. Units to Metric Equivalents			Metric Units to U.S. Equivalents		
To Convert From	Multiply By	To Get	To Convert From	Multiply By	To Get
Inches	25.4	Millimetres	Millimetres	0.0394	Inches
Inches	2.54	Centimetres	Centimetres	0.3937	Inches
Feet	30.48	Centimetres	Centimetres	0.0328	Feet
Feet	0.3048	Metres	Metres	3.2808	Feet
Yards	0.9144	Metres	Metres	1.0936	Yards
Square inches	6.4516	Square centimetres	Square centimetres	0.1550	Square inches
Square feet	0.0929	Square metres	Square metres	10.764	Square feet
Square yards	0.8361	Square metres	Square metres	1.1960	Square yards
Cubic inches	16.387	Cubic centimetres	Cubic centimetres	0.0610	Cubic inches
Cubic feet	0.0283	Cubic metres	Cubic metres	35.315	Cubic feet
Cubic feet	28.316	Litres	Litres	0.0353	Cubic feet
Cubic yards	0.7646	Cubic metres	Cubic metres	1.308	Cubic yards
Cubic yards	764.55	Litres	Litres	0.0013	Cubic yards

To convert from degrees Fahrenheit (F) to degrees Celsius (C), first subtract 32, then multiply by $\frac{5}{9}$.

To convert from degrees Celsius to degrees Fahrenheit, multiply by $\frac{9}{5}$, then add 32.